Math Expressions

Homework and Remembering • Volume 2

Developed by
The Children's Math Worlds Research Project

PROJECT DIRECTOR AND AUTHOR
Dr. Karen C. Fuson

This material is based upon work supported by the
National Science Foundation
under Grant Numbers
ESI-9816320, REC-9806020, and RED-935373.

Any opinions, findings, and conclusions, or recommendations expressed in this material
are those of the author and do not necessarily reflect the views of the National Science Foundation.

 HOUGHTON MIFFLIN HARCOURT

Teacher Reviewers

Kindergarten
Patricia Stroh Sugiyama
Wilmette, Illinois

Barbara Wahle
Evanston, Illinois

Grade 1
Sandra Budson
Newton, Massachusetts

Janet Pecci
Chicago, Illinois

Megan Rees
Chicago, Illinois

Grade 2
Molly Dunn
Danvers, Massachusetts

Agnes Lesnick
Hillside, Illinois

Rita Soto
Chicago, Illinois

Grade 3
Jane Curran
Honesdale, Pennsylvania

Sandra Tucker
Chicago, Illinois

Grade 4
Sara Stoneberg Llibre
Chicago, Illinois

Sheri Roedel
Chicago, Illinois

Grade 5
Todd Atler
Chicago, Illinois

Leah Barry
Norfolk, Massachusetts

Credits

© Kerstin Layer/Age Fotostock

Ilustrative art: Robin Boyer/Deborah Wolfe, LTD; Geoff Smith
Technical art: Nesbitt Graphics, Inc.
Photos: Nesbitt Graphics, Inc.

Homework

Home Study Sheet C

6s

Count-bys	Mixed Up ×	Mixed Up ÷
1 × 6 = 6	10 × 6 = 60	54 ÷ 6 = 9
2 × 6 = 12	8 × 6 = 48	30 ÷ 6 = 5
3 × 6 = 18	2 × 6 = 12	12 ÷ 6 = 2
4 × 6 = 24	6 × 6 = 36	60 ÷ 6 = 10
5 × 6 = 30	4 × 6 = 24	48 ÷ 6 = 8
6 × 6 = 36	1 × 6 = 6	36 ÷ 6 = 6
7 × 6 = 42	9 × 6 = 54	6 ÷ 6 = 1
8 × 6 = 48	3 × 6 = 18	42 ÷ 6 = 7
9 × 6 = 54	7 × 6 = 42	18 ÷ 6 = 3
10 × 6 = 60	5 × 6 = 30	24 ÷ 6 = 4

7s

Count-bys	Mixed Up ×	Mixed Up ÷
1 × 7 = 7	6 × 7 = 42	70 ÷ 7 = 10
2 × 7 = 14	8 × 7 = 56	14 ÷ 7 = 2
3 × 7 = 21	5 × 7 = 35	28 ÷ 7 = 4
4 × 7 = 28	9 × 7 = 63	56 ÷ 7 = 8
5 × 7 = 35	4 × 7 = 28	42 ÷ 7 = 6
6 × 7 = 42	10 × 7 = 70	63 ÷ 7 = 9
7 × 7 = 49	3 × 7 = 21	21 ÷ 7 = 3
8 × 7 = 56	1 × 7 = 7	49 ÷ 7 = 7
9 × 7 = 63	7 × 7 = 49	7 ÷ 7 = 1
10 × 7 = 70	2 × 7 = 14	35 ÷ 7 = 5

8s

Count-bys	Mixed Up ×	Mixed Up ÷
1 × 8 = 8	6 × 8 = 48	16 ÷ 8 = 2
2 × 8 = 16	10 × 8 = 80	40 ÷ 8 = 5
3 × 8 = 24	7 × 8 = 56	72 ÷ 8 = 9
4 × 8 = 32	2 × 8 = 16	32 ÷ 8 = 4
5 × 8 = 40	4 × 8 = 32	8 ÷ 8 = 1
6 × 8 = 48	8 × 8 = 64	80 ÷ 8 = 10
7 × 8 = 56	5 × 8 = 40	64 ÷ 8 = 8
8 × 8 = 64	10 × 8 = 80	24 ÷ 8 = 3
9 × 8 = 72	3 × 8 = 24	56 ÷ 8 = 7
10 × 8 = 80	1 × 8 = 8	48 ÷ 8 = 6

squares

Count-bys	Mixed Up ×	Mixed Up ÷
1 × 1 = 1	3 × 3 = 9	25 ÷ 5 = 5
2 × 2 = 4	9 × 9 = 81	4 ÷ 2 = 2
3 × 3 = 9	4 × 4 = 16	81 ÷ 9 = 9
4 × 4 = 16	6 × 6 = 36	9 ÷ 3 = 3
5 × 5 = 25	2 × 2 = 4	36 ÷ 6 = 6
6 × 6 = 36	7 × 7 = 49	100 ÷ 10 = 10
7 × 7 = 49	10 × 10 = 100	16 ÷ 4 = 4
8 × 8 = 64	1 × 1 = 1	49 ÷ 7 = 7
9 × 9 = 81	5 × 5 = 25	1 ÷ 1 = 1
10 × 10 = 100	8 × 8 = 64	64 ÷ 8 = 8

Homework

Multiply or divide to find the missing numbers. Then check your answers at the bottom of this page.

1. $6 \times 6 = \boxed{}$

2. $20 \div 4 = \boxed{}$

3. $9 * 9 = \boxed{}$

4. $32 / 4 = \boxed{}$

5. $9 \cdot \boxed{} = 54$

6. $\dfrac{30}{10} = \boxed{}$

7. $5 \times 0 = \boxed{}$

8. $\dfrac{48}{6} = \boxed{}$

9. $3 \times 6 = \boxed{}$

10. $6\overline{)30}$

11. $8 \cdot 4 = \boxed{}$

12. $12 \div 6 = \boxed{}$

13. $6 * \boxed{} = 42$

14. $\dfrac{6}{6} = \boxed{}$

15. $3 \cdot 4 = \boxed{}$

16. $15 / 5 = \boxed{}$

17. $10 \div 10 = \boxed{}$

18. $2 * 7 = \boxed{}$

19. $\boxed{} \times 2 = 10$

20. $6\overline{)18}$

21. $10 \times \boxed{} = 70$

12. 2 13. 7 14. 1 15. 12 16. 3 17. 1 18. 14 19. 5 20. 3 21. 7

1. 36 2. 5 3. 81 4. 8 5. 6 6. 3 7. 0 8. 8 9. 18 10. 5 11. 32

Solve Area Word Problems

Name _____ **Date** _____

Homework

Study Plan	
	_____
	Homework Helper

Complete each Missing Number puzzle.

1.

×			6
9	36		
2			
	12	9	

2.

×	7		6
	28		24
6		30	
	56		48

3.

×			4
5		30	
7	56	42	
			12

Solve each problem. Label your answers with the correct units.

4. Raul built a rectangular tabletop with a length of 3 feet and a width of 6 feet. What is the area of the tabletop?

_____

5. Li Fong covered the rectangular floor of his tree house with 48 square feet of carpeting. If one side of the floor has a length of 6 feet, what is the length of the adjacent side?

_____

6. Frances wants to paint a rectangular wall that has a width of 8 feet and a height of 9 feet. She has a quart of paint that will cover 85 square feet. What is the area of the wall? Does Frances have enough paint?

_____

7. Willis cut out a paper rectangle with an area of 42 square centimeters. If one side has a length of 6 centimeters, what is the length of the adjacent side?

_____

Name _____ **Date** _____

Remembering

Subtract.

1. $1,000 - 644 =$ _____
2. $482 - 138 =$ _____
3. $303 - 161 =$ _____

4. $400 - 236 =$ _____
5. $855 - 77 =$ _____
6. $362 - 186 =$ _____

Circle every word that describes each figure.

7.

quadrilateral

parallelogram

rectangle

square

8.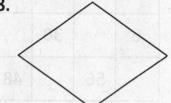

quadrilateral

parallelogram

rectangle

square

9.

quadrilateral

parallelogram

rectangle

square

Write an equation to solve the problem.

10. Last winter, Emily earned money by shoveling snow from her neighbors' driveways. She charged $9 for each driveway. She shoveled 8 driveways. How much money did she earn?

_____

11. Brigitte has a collection of CDs for a party. She can put 5 CDs in the CD player at one time. If she has 15 CDs, how many times can she change all the CDs?

_____

Solve Area Word Problems

Homework

Use this chart to practice your 8s count-bys, multiplications, and divisions. Then have your Homework Helper test you.

	× In Order	× Mixed Up	÷ Mixed Up
8s	$1 \times 8 = 8$	$3 \times 8 = 24$	$40 \div 8 = 5$
	$2 \times 8 = 16$	$9 \times 8 = 72$	$56 \div 8 = 7$
	$3 \times 8 = 24$	$6 \times 8 = 48$	$24 \div 8 = 3$
	$4 \times 8 = 32$	$4 \times 8 = 32$	$72 \div 8 = 9$
	$5 \times 8 = 40$	$2 \times 8 = 16$	$8 \div 8 = 1$
	$6 \times 8 = 48$	$8 \times 8 = 64$	$48 \div 8 = 6$
	$7 \times 8 = 56$	$1 \times 8 = 8$	$32 \div 8 = 4$
	$8 \times 8 = 64$	$5 \times 8 = 40$	$64 \div 8 = 8$
	$9 \times 8 = 72$	$10 \times 8 = 80$	$16 \div 8 = 2$
	$10 \times 8 = 80$	$7 \times 8 = 56$	$80 \div 8 = 10$

Homework

Name   **Date**

Home Check Sheet 8: 6s and 8s

6s Multiplications	6s Divisions	8s Multiplications	8s Divisions
$10 \times 6 = 60$	$24 / 6 = 4$	$2 \times 8 = 16$	$72 / 8 = 9$
$6 \cdot 4 = 24$	$48 \div 6 = 8$	$8 \cdot 10 = 80$	$16 \div 8 = 2$
$6 * 7 = 42$	$60 / 6 = 10$	$3 * 8 = 24$	$40 / 8 = 5$
$2 \times 6 = 12$	$12 \div 6 = 2$	$9 \times 8 = 72$	$8 \div 8 = 1$
$6 \cdot 5 = 30$	$42 / 6 = 7$	$8 \cdot 4 = 32$	$80 / 8 = 10$
$6 * 8 = 48$	$30 \div 6 = 5$	$8 * 7 = 56$	$48 \div 8 = 6$
$9 \times 6 = 54$	$6 / 6 = 1$	$5 \times 8 = 40$	$56 / 8 = 7$
$6 \cdot 1 = 6$	$18 \div 6 = 3$	$8 \cdot 6 = 48$	$24 \div 8 = 3$
$6 * 6 = 36$	$54 / 6 = 9$	$1 * 8 = 8$	$64 / 8 = 8$
$6 \times 3 = 18$	$36 / 6 = 6$	$8 \times 8 = 64$	$32 / 8 = 4$
$6 \cdot 6 = 36$	$48 \div 6 = 8$	$4 \cdot 8 = 32$	$80 \div 8 = 10$
$5 * 6 = 30$	$12 / 6 = 2$	$6 * 8 = 48$	$56 / 8 = 7$
$6 \times 2 = 12$	$24 \div 6 = 4$	$8 \times 3 = 24$	$8 \div 8 = 1$
$4 \cdot 6 = 24$	$60 / 6 = 10$	$7 \cdot 8 = 56$	$24 / 8 = 3$
$6 * 9 = 54$	$6 \div 6 = 1$	$8 * 2 = 16$	$64 \div 8 = 8$
$8 \times 6 = 48$	$42 / 6 = 7$	$8 \times 9 = 72$	$16 / 8 = 2$
$7 \cdot 6 = 42$	$18 \div 6 = 3$	$8 \cdot 1 = 8$	$72 \div 8 = 9$
$6 * 10 = 60$	$36 \div 6 = 6$	$8 * 8 = 64$	$32 \div 8 = 4$
$1 \times 6 = 6$	$30 / 6 = 5$	$10 \times 8 = 80$	$40 / 8 = 5$
$4 \cdot 6 = 24$	$54 \div 6 = 9$	$5 \cdot 8 = 40$	$48 \div 8 = 6$

Study Plan
Homework Helper

Find the missing number in each Fast-Array Drawing.

1.

2.

3.

Complete each function table.

4. In this function table, the numbers in the N row are in order.

N	1	2	3			6	7		9	10
N * 4		8		16	20	24		32		

5. In this function table, the numbers in the N row are out of order.

N	2		5	9		10	4		3	8
N * 8	16	56		72	8			48		

Solve.

6. Joseph gave his 6 nephews $48 for helping him clean out the garage. The boys divided the money equally. How much money did each boy get?

_____

7. Miki has 3 planting boxes for her flowers. Each box is 4 feet wide and 8 feet long. How much area for planting flowers does Miki have altogether?

_____

Name _____ **Date** _____

Remembering

Find each sum or difference using mental math.

1. 2,400 − 800 = _____   **2.** 320 − 140 = _____   **3.** 4,000 − 3,700 = _____

4. 860 − 470 = _____   **5.** 2,200 − 300 = _____   **6.** 270 − 90 = _____

7. 16 + 8 = _____   **8.** 64 + 8 = _____   **9.** 48 + 8 = _____

10. 32 − 8 = _____   **11.** 56 − 8 = _____   **12.** 72 − 8 = _____

Solve each problem. Label your answers.

Show your work.

13. Jon ordered a book online. It took 2 weeks and 4 days for the book to arrive. How many days did Jon wait for the book?

_____

14. Three girls brought eggs on the scouting campout. Lydia and Tara each brought a dozen eggs, and Kate brought half a dozen. How many eggs did they bring in all?

_____

15. At his auto shop on Monday, Lucas changed the tires on 8 cars. How many tires did he change on Monday?

_____

16. A spider has 8 legs. How many legs are on 3 spiders?

_____

Multiply and Divide with 8

Name   **Date**

Homework

Use this chart to practice your 7s count-bys, multiplications, and divisions. Then have your Homework Helper test you.

7s	× In Order	× Mixed Up	÷ Mixed Up
	$1 \times 7 = 7$	$5 \times 7 = 35$	$56 \div 7 = 8$
	$2 \times 7 = 14$	$1 \times 7 = 7$	$42 \div 7 = 6$
	$3 \times 7 = 21$	$10 \times 7 = 70$	$14 \div 7 = 2$
	$4 \times 7 = 28$	$2 \times 7 = 14$	$7 \div 7 = 1$
	$5 \times 7 = 35$	$9 \times 7 = 63$	$70 \div 7 = 10$
	$6 \times 7 = 42$	$3 \times 7 = 21$	$49 \div 7 = 7$
	$7 \times 7 = 49$	$8 \times 7 = 56$	$21 \div 7 = 3$
	$8 \times 7 = 56$	$4 \times 7 = 28$	$35 \div 7 = 5$
	$9 \times 7 = 63$	$7 \times 7 = 49$	$63 \div 7 = 9$
	$10 \times 7 = 70$	$6 \times 7 = 42$	$28 \div 7 = 4$

Homework

Name _____   **Date** _____

Multiply or divide to find the missing numbers. Then check your answers at the bottom of this page.

1. $7 \times 7 = \boxed{}$

2. $\dfrac{64}{8} = \boxed{}$

3. $5 \times 5 = \boxed{}$

4. $28 / 7 = \boxed{}$

5. $9 \bullet \boxed{} = 27$

6. $\dfrac{48}{6} = \boxed{}$

7. $\boxed{} \times 9 = 63$

8. $7\overline{)56}$

9. $10 \times \boxed{} = 30$

10. $8 \times 5 = \boxed{}$

11. $21 \div 3 = \boxed{}$

12. $9 * 2 = \boxed{}$

13. $30 / 6 = \boxed{}$

14. $8 \bullet 5 = \boxed{}$

15. $24 \div 3 = \boxed{}$

16. $3\overline{)21}$

17. $90 \div 9 = \boxed{}$

18. $2 * 7 = \boxed{}$

19. $6 * \boxed{} = 42$

20. $\dfrac{10}{2} = \boxed{}$

21. $3 \bullet 9 = \boxed{}$

1. 49 **2.** 8 **3.** 25 **4.** 4 **5.** 3 **6.** 8 **7.** 7 **8.** 8 **9.** 3 **10.** 40 **11.** 7
12. 18 **13.** 5 **14.** 40 **15.** 8 **16.** 7 **17.** 10 **18.** 14 **19.** 7 **20.** 5 **21.** 27

Multiply and Divide with 7

Name _____ **Date** _____

Homework

Fill in the missing number in each Fast-Array Drawing.

1. 7
   21

2. 9
   5

3.
   5 35

4. 9
   8

5. 9
   45

6.
   7 49

Solve. Label your answers.

7. Rachel plans to fence in an area 7 meters long by 7 meters wide for her dog to run in. How much area will her dog have to run in?

8. Shondra has 21 tropical fish. If she divides them evenly among 3 tanks, how many fish will be in each tank?

_____

9. Write a word problem that involves multiplication. Write your problem on a sheet of paper for your teacher to use on Word Problem Day.

Name _____ **Date** _____

Remembering

Draw two different bill and coin combinations for each amount.

1. $8.86

2. $1.40

Use mental math to find the answer.

3. 14 + 7 = _____

4. 49 + 7 = _____

5. 56 + 7 = _____

6. 35 − 7 = _____

7. 63 − 7 = _____

8. 21 − 7 = _____

Use the picture to answer problems 9–13.

9. Julian wants to rent a snorkel and fins for an hour. How much will it cost?

_____

10. Ms. Thomas wants to rent a float for each of her 3 children for an hour. How much will she have to pay?

_____

Kali Beach Rental Shop

Prices are for 1-hour rentals

Snorkel	$1.50
Fins	$1.50
Wetsuit	$2.00
Float	$2.50
Paddle Boat	$4.00
Canoe	$4.50

11. Rashid is renting a wetsuit and a canoe for an hour. He pays with a $10 bill. How much change does he receive?

_____

12. Allegra and Sarah want to rent a paddleboat and 2 wetsuits for 2 hours. What will they be charged?

_____

13. Mali plans to rent a canoe for 4 hours. How much change will she receive if she pays for the rental with a $20 bill?

_____

Multiply and Divide with 7

Name _____ **Date** _____

Homework

Study Plan

Homework Helper

Complete the comparison statements.

> Sam has 18 marbles. Brenna has 3 marbles.

1. Write a comparison statement about the marbles using the word *more*.

   _____

2. Write a comparison statement about the marbles using the word *fewer*.

   _____

3. Brenna has _____ as many marbles as Sam.

4. Sam has _____ as many marbles as Brenna.

> Tara swam 5 laps at the pool. Canyon swam 15 laps.

5. Canyon swam _____ as many laps as Tara.

6. Tara swam _____ as many laps as Canyon.

Solve.

7. Mia sold 9 calendars. Ellen sold 3 times as many calendars. How many calendars did Ellen sell?

   _____

8. Alfredo walked 24 miles in the walk-a-thon. His friend Terence walked $\frac{1}{3}$ as many miles. How many miles did Terence walk?

   _____

Name _____ **Date** _____

Remembering

Solve.

Isaac drew this large rectangle, which is made up of two small rectangles.

1. Find the area of the large rectangle by finding the areas of the two small rectangles and adding them.

   _____

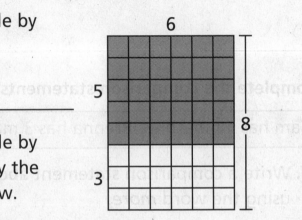

2. Find the area of the large rectangle by multiplying the number of rows by the number of square units in each row.

   _____

Use the bar graph to solve problems 3–6.

Trees in Caspian's Orchard

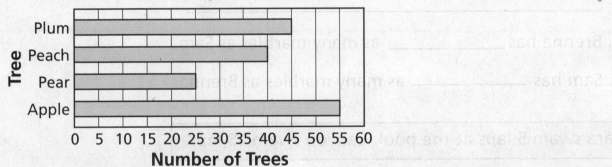

3. How many more peach trees than pear trees are in Caspian's orchard?

   _____

4. How many pear and apple trees are in Caspian's orchard altogether?

   _____

5. How many plum, peach, and pear trees are in Caspian's orchard?

   _____

6. Write a problem using the information from the bar graph. Solve your problem.

Comparison Word Problems

Name _____ **Date** _____

Homework

Study Plan

_____

Homework Helper

Complete the sentence.

Kristi is training for a marathon. This month she ran 36 miles. Last month she ran only 6 miles.

Show your work.

1. Kristi ran _____ as many miles this month as last month.

2. Kristi ran _____ as many miles last month as this month.

Make a drawing to help you solve each problem.

3. Darnell swam 8 miles last month. He plans to swim 3 times as many miles this month. How many miles does he plan to swim this month?

   _____

4. Geoff rode 64 miles on his bike last month. He rode $\frac{1}{8}$ as many miles this month as last month. How many miles did he ride this month?

   _____

5. Molly ran in 4 races at the track meet. Her sister Sophie ran in 8 races. How many times more races did Sophie run in than Molly? _____

6. Tamara made 8 baskets in the championship game. Lucia made $\frac{1}{4}$ as many baskets as Tamara. How many baskets did Lucia make? _____

Name _____ **Date** _____

Remembering

Subtract.

1. 408 − 275 = _____ **2.** 129 − 63 = _____ **3.** 472 − 319 = _____

4. 647 − 118 = _____ **5.** 727 − 144 = _____ **6.** 300 − 17 = _____

Find the area and perimeter of each rectangle.

7. 7 ft
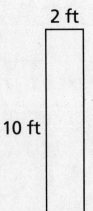
3 ft

_____

_____

8. 5 cm

4 cm

_____

_____

9. 6 in.

6 in.

_____

_____

10. 2 ft

10 ft

_____

_____

11. 3 cm

7 cm

_____

_____

12. 7 in.
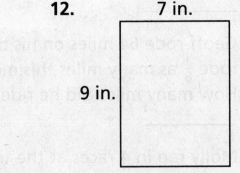
9 in.

_____

_____

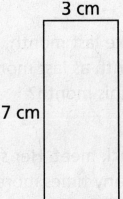

More Comparison Word Problems

Homework

Home Check Sheet 9: 7s and Squares

7s Multiplications	7s Divisions	Squares Multiplications	Squares Divisions
$4 \times 7 = 28$	$14 / 7 = 2$	$8 \times 8 = 64$	$81 / 9 = 9$
$7 \cdot 2 = 14$	$28 \div 7 = 4$	$10 \cdot 10 = 100$	$4 \div 2 = 2$
$7 * 8 = 56$	$70 / 7 = 10$	$3 * 3 = 9$	$25 / 5 = 5$
$7 \times 7 = 49$	$56 \div 7 = 8$	$9 \times 9 = 81$	$1 \div 1 = 1$
$7 \cdot 1 = 7$	$42 / 7 = 6$	$4 \cdot 4 = 16$	$100 / 10 = 10$
$7 * 10 = 70$	$63 \div 7 = 9$	$7 * 7 = 49$	$36 \div 6 = 6$
$3 \times 7 = 21$	$7 / 7 = 1$	$5 \times 5 = 25$	$49 / 7 = 7$
$7 \cdot 6 = 42$	$49 \div 7 = 7$	$6 \cdot 6 = 36$	$9 \div 3 = 3$
$5 * 7 = 35$	$21 / 7 = 3$	$1 * 1 = 1$	$64 / 8 = 8$
$7 \times 9 = 63$	$35 / 7 = 5$	$5 * 5 = 25$	$16 / 4 = 4$
$7 \cdot 4 = 28$	$7 \div 7 = 1$	$1 \cdot 1 = 1$	$100 \div 10 = 10$
$9 * 7 = 63$	$63 / 7 = 9$	$3 \cdot 3 = 9$	$49 / 7 = 7$
$2 \times 7 = 14$	$14 \div 7 = 2$	$10 \times 10 = 100$	$1 \div 1 = 1$
$7 \cdot 5 = 35$	$70 / 7 = 10$	$4 \times 4 = 16$	$9 / 3 = 3$
$8 * 7 = 56$	$21 \div 7 = 3$	$9 * 9 = 81$	$64 \div 8 = 8$
$7 \times 3 = 21$	$49 / 7 = 7$	$2 \times 2 = 4$	$4 / 2 = 2$
$6 \cdot 7 = 42$	$28 \div 7 = 4$	$6 * 6 = 36$	$81 \div 9 = 9$
$10 * 7 = 70$	$56 \div 7 = 8$	$7 \times 7 = 49$	$16 \div 4 = 4$
$1 \times 7 = 7$	$35 / 7 = 5$	$5 \cdot 5 = 25$	$25 / 5 = 5$
$7 \cdot 7 = 49$	$42 \div 7 = 6$	$8 \cdot 8 = 64$	$36 \div 6 = 6$

Name _____   **Date** _____

Homework

Multiply or divide to find the unknown numbers. Then check your answers at the bottom of this page.

1. ☐ × 6 = 48

2. 56 ÷ 7 = ☐

3. 10 × ☐ = 90

4. 64 / 8 = ☐

5. 9 • ☐ = 63

6. $\frac{25}{5}$ = ☐

7. 8 × 9 = ☐

8. 9)$\overline{36}$ ☐

9. 7 * 7 = ☐

10. 6 * ☐ = 36

11. $\frac{32}{4}$ = ☐

12. 3 • 3 = ☐

13. 30 / 6 = ☐

14. 16 ÷ 4 = ☐

15. 8 * 5 = ☐

16. 6 × 4 = ☐

17. $\frac{81}{9}$ = ☐

18. 5 × 7 = ☐

19. 60 / 6 = ☐

20. 7 • 8 = ☐

21. 42 ÷ 7 = ☐

22. 6)$\overline{54}$ ☐

23. 32 ÷ 8 = ☐

24. 9 * 9 = ☐

23. 4 24. 81

13. 5 14. 4 15. 40 16. 24 17. 9 18. 35 19. 10 20. 56 21. 6 22. 9

1. 8 2. 8 3. 9 4. 8 5. 7 6. 5 7. 72 8. 4 9. 49 10. 6 11. 8 12. 9

Square Numbers

Name _____ **Date** _____

Homework

Write a multiplication equation for each square array.

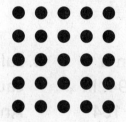

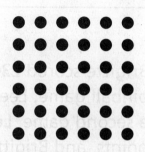

1. _____ 2. _____ 3. _____

Solve.

4. Julia used 1 foot square stone tiles to make a patio. She laid the tiles in a square, 7 tiles wide by 7 tiles long. What is the area of Julia's new patio?

_____

5. Sal brought 2 dozen apples to a science club meeting. He divided the apples equally among the 8 people there. How many apples did he give each person?

_____

6. Lehie has 21 crystals in her collection. Her brother Tomer has 7 crystals. How many more crystals does Lehie have than Tomer?

_____

7. Emmanuel collected 49 leaves last week. He collected the same number of leaves each day. How many leaves did he collect on Monday?

_____

Complete.

8.

×	6	4	
	24		32

9.

×		4	
9	45		81

10.

×	8		3
8		56	

Remembering

Solve.

1. Isabel had $37. She bought 2 CDs for $11 each. Then she earned some money babysitting. Now she has $53. How much did she earn babysitting?

_____

2. Arnon planted 4 apple trees and 7 peach trees. Jenn planted 5 more apple trees than Arnon and 4 fewer peach trees. How many trees did Jenn plant in all?

_____

3. Brigitte scored 234 points in a pinball game. Lee scored 394. In a second game, Lee scored 164 points, and Brigitte scored 307 points. Altogether, who scored the most points? How many more?

_____

4. Julian caught 8 fish, Tana caught 6, Stewart caught 11, and Ana caught 4. They threw the 9 smallest fish back into the water. Then they each caught 2 more fish. How many fish do they have now?

_____

Draw 2 rectangles that each have a perimeter of 12 centimeters. Write the area inside each figure.

5.

Square Numbers

Homework

Home Check Sheet 10: 6s, 7s, and 8s

6s, 7s, and 8s Multiplications	6s, 7s, and 8s Multiplications	6s, 7s, and 8s Divisions	6s, 7s, and 8s Divisions
$1 \times 6 = 6$	$0 \times 8 = 0$	$24 / 6 = 4$	$54 / 6 = 9$
$6 \cdot 7 = 42$	$6 \cdot 2 = 12$	$21 \div 7 = 3$	$24 \div 8 = 3$
$3 * 8 = 24$	$4 * 7 = 28$	$16 / 8 = 2$	$14 / 7 = 2$
$6 \times 2 = 12$	$8 \times 3 = 24$	$24 \div 8 = 3$	$32 \div 8 = 4$
$7 \cdot 5 = 35$	$5 \cdot 6 = 30$	$14 / 7 = 2$	$18 / 6 = 3$
$8 * 4 = 32$	$7 * 2 = 14$	$30 \div 6 = 5$	$56 \div 7 = 8$
$6 \times 6 = 36$	$3 \times 8 = 24$	$35 / 7 = 5$	$40 / 8 = 5$
$8 \cdot 7 = 56$	$6 \cdot 4 = 24$	$24 \div 8 = 3$	$35 \div 7 = 5$
$9 * 8 = 72$	$0 * 7 = 0$	$18 / 6 = 3$	$12 / 6 = 2$
$6 \times 10 = 60$	$8 \times 1 = 8$	$12 / 6 = 2$	$21 / 7 = 3$
$7 \cdot 1 = 7$	$8 \cdot 6 = 48$	$42 \div 7 = 6$	$16 \div 8 = 2$
$8 * 3 = 24$	$7 * 9 = 63$	$56 / 8 = 7$	$42 / 6 = 7$
$5 \times 6 = 30$	$10 \times 8 = 80$	$49 \div 7 = 7$	$80 \div 8 = 10$
$4 \cdot 7 = 28$	$6 \cdot 10 = 60$	$16 / 8 = 2$	$36 / 6 = 6$
$2 * 8 = 16$	$3 * 7 = 21$	$60 \div 6 = 10$	$7 \div 7 = 1$
$7 \times 7 = 49$	$8 \times 4 = 32$	$54 / 6 = 9$	$64 / 8 = 8$
$7 \cdot 6 = 42$	$6 \cdot 5 = 30$	$8 \div 8 = 1$	$24 \div 6 = 4$
$8 * 8 = 64$	$7 * 4 = 28$	$28 \div 7 = 4$	$21 \div 7 = 3$
$9 \times 6 = 54$	$8 \times 8 = 64$	$72 / 8 = 9$	$49 / 7 = 7$
$10 \cdot 7 = 70$	$6 \cdot 9 = 54$	$56 \div 7 = 8$	$24 \div 8 = 3$

Name   Date

Home Check Sheet 11: 0s–10s

0s–10s Multiplications	0s–10s Multiplications	0s–10s Divisions	0s–10s Divisions
$9 \times 0 = 0$	$9 \times 4 = 36$	$9 / 1 = 9$	$90 / 10 = 9$
$1 \cdot 1 = 1$	$5 \cdot 9 = 45$	$12 \div 3 = 4$	$64 \div 8 = 8$
$2 * 3 = 6$	$6 * 10 = 60$	$14 / 2 = 7$	$15 / 5 = 3$
$1 \times 3 = 3$	$7 \times 3 = 21$	$20 \div 4 = 5$	$12 \div 6 = 2$
$5 \cdot 4 = 20$	$5 \cdot 3 = 15$	$10 / 5 = 2$	$14 / 7 = 2$
$7 * 5 = 35$	$4 * 1 = 4$	$48 \div 8 = 6$	$45 \div 9 = 5$
$6 \times 9 = 54$	$7 \times 5 = 35$	$35 / 7 = 5$	$8 / 1 = 8$
$0 \cdot 7 = 0$	$6 \cdot 3 = 18$	$60 \div 6 = 10$	$30 \div 3 = 10$
$1 * 8 = 8$	$8 * 7 = 56$	$81 / 9 = 9$	$16 / 4 = 4$
$9 \times 8 = 72$	$5 \times 8 = 40$	$20 / 10 = 2$	$8 / 2 = 4$
$2 \cdot 10 = 20$	$9 \cdot 9 = 81$	$16 \div 2 = 8$	$80 \div 10 = 8$
$0 * 7 = 0$	$9 * 10 = 90$	$30 / 5 = 6$	$36 / 4 = 9$
$4 \times 1 = 4$	$0 \times 0 = 0$	$49 \div 7 = 7$	$25 \div 5 = 5$
$2 \cdot 4 = 8$	$1 \cdot 0 = 0$	$60 / 6 = 10$	$42 / 7 = 6$
$10 * 3 = 30$	$1 * 6 = 6$	$30 \div 3 = 10$	$36 \div 6 = 6$
$8 \times 4 = 32$	$7 \times 2 = 14$	$8 / 1 = 8$	$90 / 9 = 10$
$5 \cdot 8 = 40$	$6 \cdot 3 = 18$	$16 \div 4 = 4$	$24 \div 8 = 3$
$4 * 6 = 24$	$4 * 5 = 20$	$16 \div 8 = 2$	$6 \div 2 = 3$
$7 \times 0 = 0$	$6 \times 6 = 36$	$40 / 10 = 4$	$9 / 3 = 3$
$1 \cdot 8 = 8$	$10 \cdot 7 = 70$	$36 \div 9 = 4$	$1 \div 1 = 1$

Study Plan

Homework Helper

Solve.

1. Sarah's chickens laid 3 dozen eggs over the weekend. She divided them equally into cartons to give away to her 6 closest neighbors. How many eggs did she put in each carton?

2. Latisha needs 60 square feet of cloth. She has a rectangular piece of cloth that measures 3 ft by 9 ft, and a square piece that measures 5 ft on a side. Does she have enough cloth? If not, how much more does she need?

Complete each function table.

3.

N	2		3	7		8	9		5
6 * N		36			60	48		6		24

4.

N		10	6	3			7	5		1
N * 7	28				56	14			63	

Fill in the missing number in each Fast-Array.

5.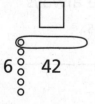

6 | 42

6.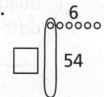

6

54

7.

8

7 | □

Remembering

Solve each problem.

1. Elora had $2.53. She earned some money selling her old books and toys at a yard sale. Now she has $9.09. How much money did she earn at the yard sale?

   _____

2. Malie and Meghan collect crystals. Together they have 376 crystals. Malie has 149 crystals. How many does Meghan have?

   _____

3. One thousand two hundred thirty three people started the Austin Marathon. Some people weren't able to finish the marathon. 783 people completed the marathon. How many people did not finish?

   _____

4. Park Side School students raised money by collecting some used ink cartridges last year. They collected 478 ink cartridges this year. They collected 1,234 cartridges in those two years. How many cartridges were collected last year?

   _____

Tell whether each statement is true or false. Make sketches if you find it helpful.

5. If you know the length of one side of any quadrilateral, you can find the quadrilateral's perimeter.

   _____

6. If you know the lengths of two *adjacent* sides of a rectangle, you can find its perimeter.

   _____

7. If you know the lengths of two *opposite* sides of a rectangle, you can find its perimeter.

   _____

8. The adjacent sides of a quadrilateral are always different lengths.

   _____

Practice with 6s, 7s, and 8s

Study Plan

Homework Helper

Solve each problem. Write an equation to show what you did.

1. Robert planted 7 trees behind Westwood School. He planted 6 times as many trees in front of the school. How many trees did he plant in front?

_____

2. Nelson collected 58 cans of food during his town's food drive. Michael collected 67 cans of food. How many cans of food did they collect altogether?

3. On a snorkeling trip, Betina spotted 27 different kinds of fish. Her younger sister Lucia spotted one third as many. How many different kinds of fish did Lucia spot?

_____

4. Arnon earned $27 delivering newspapers last week. He spent $9 on a book about snakes. How much money does he have left?

_____

Write a question to finish each word problem. Then solve the problem.

5. Sonya has 272 coins in her collection. Her brother Erez has 298 coins.

Question: _____

_____ Solution: _____

6. Richard folded 32 shirts and stacked them in 4 equal piles.

Question: _____

_____ Solution: _____

Remembering

Round each number to the nearest ten.

1. 94 _____ 2. 309 _____ 3. 82 _____ 4. 888 _____

Round each number to the nearest hundred.

5. 192 _____ 6. 538 _____ 7. 389 _____ 8. 856 _____

Solve each problem.

9. Pedro's class cut out 314 paper snowflakes to decorate their classroom. Natalie's class cut out 229 snowflakes. How many fewer snowflakes did Natalie's class make?

_____

10. Kai and Marcia spent Saturday doing jigsaw puzzles. They put together puzzles with 500 pieces, 1,200 pieces, and 150 pieces. How many puzzle pieces did they put together in all?

_____

Fill in the missing number in each Fast Array drawing.

11.

12.

13.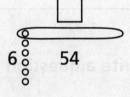

14.

15.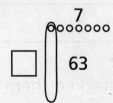

16.

Solve Mixed Word Problems

Homework

```
┌─────────────────────────────────────────────────────┐
│ Study Plan                                           │
│                                                      │
│                                                      │
│                                  _____    │
│                                  Homework Helper     │
│                                                      │
└─────────────────────────────────────────────────────┘
```

Solve each problem.

1. The tour boats at the Laguna can carry 8 passengers. Jacob watched 6 boats float by. Three of the boats had 2 empty seats. The others were full. How many passengers were on the 6 boats?

_____

2. Jerome bought 8 packs of baseball cards at a garage sale. Each pack had 10 cards. He gave his younger sister 3 cards from each pack. How many cards does Jerome have left?

_____

3. Zoe cut a pan of brownies into 5 rows and 6 columns. She gave 6 brownies to her family, and divided the rest evenly among the 8 people at her scout meeting. How many brownies did each person at her scout meeting get?

_____

4. Four girls helped Mr. Day plant a garden. For their help, he gave the girls $24 to share equally. Later, Mrs. Day gave each girl $2 for helping to clean up. How much money did each girl get?

_____

5. Grace made 7 bouquets for the bridesmaids in a wedding. She put 3 roses, 4 tulips, and 2 lilies in each bouquet. How many flowers did she use in all?

_____

6. Takala put 9 marbles in the box, Jackie put in 7, and Laird put in 11. Then they divided the marbles evenly among themselves. How many did each person get?

_____

Remembering

Solve each problem by rounding to the nearest hundred.

1. The population of Westville is 783. The population of Eastville is 327. About how many people live in the two towns altogether?

_____

2. Of the 1,822 people who attended the county fair, 178 saw the horse show. About how many fairgoers did not see the horse show?

_____

Use the graph to solve problems 3–8.

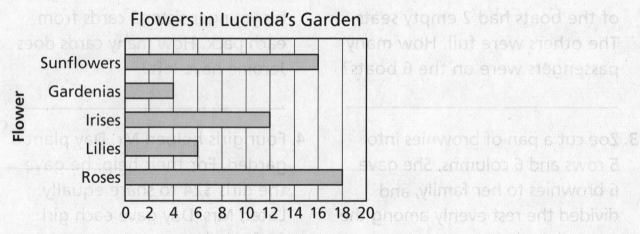

Flowers in Lucinda's Garden

3. Lucinda has _____ as many roses as lilies.

4. Lucinda has _____ as many gardenias as irises.

5. Lucinda has _____ as many sunflowers as gardenias.

6. Lucinda has _____ as many lilies as irises.

7. Lucinda has _____ more irises than lilies.

8. Lucinda has _____ fewer gardenias than sunflowers.

    Solve Multi-Step Word Problems

Study Plan

Homework Helper

Solve each problem.

1. Shamariah collects silk roses. She had 17 silk roses in a vase. Six friends each gave her 3 more roses. How many roses does Shamariah have now?

2. Robin has 42 quarters. Jay has 1/7 as many quarters as Robin has. Tori has 4 times as many quarters as Jay. How many quarters does Tori have?

3. A pet store had 9 corn snakes. 7 of the snakes laid 8 eggs each. All but 5 of the eggs hatched. How many corn snakes does the pet store have now?

4. In a paper airplane contest, Amanda's plane flew 19 ft farther than Darren's plane. Darren's plane flew twice as far as Rachel's plane. Rachel's plane flew 23 ft. How far did Amanda's plane fly?

5. Jenna divided 120 daisies into 2 equal groups. Then she divided one group equally into 10 small bunches, and she divided the other group equally into 6 large bunches. She gave her grandmother one large bunch and one small bunch. How many daisies did Jenna give her grandmother?

Remembering

Find the amount of change by counting on to the amount paid. Draw the coins and bills you count on with.

1. Pablo paid for a $3.89 salad with four $1 bills. How much change did he get? _____

2. Aleta bought 2 puzzle magazines for $1.61 each. She gave the cashier a $5 bill and a quarter. How much change did she get? _____

3. Sara paid for $18.12 worth of groceries with a $20 bill. How much change did she get? _____

4. Ahmad bought 3 pears for $0.79 each. He paid with three $1 bills. How much change did he get? _____

5. Use the information in this table to complete the horizontal bar graph.

José's Bird-Watching Trip

Bird	Number Sighted
American Bald Eagle	40
Falcon	15
Great Horned Owl	20

Solve Complex Multi-Step Word Problems

Study Plan

Homework Helper

Solve each problem.

1. Julia used square tiles to make a design. She laid the tiles in a square, 8 tiles wide by 8 tiles long. Each tile has an area of 1 square inch. What is the area of Julia's tile design?

_____

2. Bart lives 6 blocks from his grandparents. Melinda lives 8 times as far from her grandparents as Bart does. How many blocks does Melinda live from her grandparents?

_____

3. Rose rode the roller coaster 9 times. Leila rode the roller coaster $\frac{1}{3}$ as many times as Rose. Joseph rode the roller coaster 8 times as many times as Leila. How many more times did Joseph ride the roller coaster than Rose?

_____

4. Shondra has 72 roses and 48 lilies. She wants to make 8 bouquets with them, with the same number of each type of flower in each bouquet. How many flowers will be in each bouquet?

_____

5. Willis wants to paint two walls in a room. The ceiling is 8 feet high. One wall is 8 feet wide, and the other 9 feet wide. He has 2 quarts of paint that will each cover 75 square feet. What is the area of the walls he wants to paint? Does he have enough paint?

_____

6. Randall bought 7 computer games at a yard sale. He paid $4 each for 4 of the games, and $5 each for the rest. How much money did he spend?

_____

Remembering

Complete each equation.

1. 27 + 127 = _____

2. 243 − 89 = _____

3. _____ + 109 = 157

4. 823 − 644 = _____

5. 632 − _____ = 81

6. 227 + 46 = _____

Use the price list to solve problems 7–12.

Sunflower School's
Blowout Yard Sale Fundraiser

books $\quad$ puzzles $\quad$ games $\quad$ toys
50¢ $\qquad$ $1.00 $\qquad$ $1.50 $\qquad$ 75¢

roller blades $\qquad$ skateboards
$4.50 $\qquad\qquad$ $3.75

7. Jon bought a skateboard and a toy at the yard sale. How much did he spend?

_____

8. Laura bought 2 games, a book, and a pair of roller blades. How much did she spend?

_____

9. Jessie bought 3 toys. She paid with a $5 bill. How much change did she receive?

_____

10. Macy bought 2 books, a game, and a toy. How much did she spend?

_____

11. Geri has $9. She wants to buy 2 skateboards. Will she have enough left over to buy 2 puzzles as well?

_____

12. Alfredo has a $10 bill. He wants to buy a skateboard and a pair of roller blades. Will he have enough left over to buy a game?

_____

Homework

Connections

How could you use the fact that
$8 \times 7 = 56$ to find the product of
8×14?

_____

_____

_____

_____

_____

Reasoning and Proof

Tam has some dimes in her piggy
bank. She has no other coins. Could
she have exactly 45¢ in her piggy
bank? Explain.

_____

_____

_____

_____

Communication

Would you rather have 0×9
dollars or 1×3 dollars? Explain.

_____

_____

_____

_____

Representation

On grid paper, draw a rectangle
that is 17 units by 3 units. Break the
rectangle into two smaller rectangles.
How can finding the area of the two
smaller rectangles help you find the
area of the larger rectangle?

_____

_____

_____

_____

_____

_____

_____

_____

Name _____ **Date** _____

Remembering

Complete each equation.

1. 35 + 149 = ☐   **2.** ☐ + 123 = 197   **3.** 356 − 78 = ☐

4. 731 − 256 = ☐   **5.** 347 + 29 = ☐   **6.** 541 − ☐ = 491

Find the amount of change by counting on from the amount paid. Draw the coins and bills you count on with.

7. Melvin bought a sandwich for $4.76. He paid with a $5 bill. How much change did he get?

_____

8. Bala bought 2 books for $4.67 each. She gave the cashier a $10 bill. How much change did she get? _____

Use the "Fruit For Sale" sign to solve problems 9–10.

Fruit for Sale

Apple   50¢
Apple Cider $1.50
Orange Juice $1.25

9. Pedro bought an apple and orange juice. How much did he spend? _____

10. Linda bought 2 cups of apple cider. How much did she spend? _____

       Use Mathematical Processes

Homework

Write the time on the digital clock. Then write how to say the time.

1.
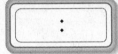
_____

2.
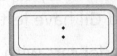
_____

3.

_____

4.
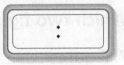
_____

Draw the hands on the anolog clock. Write the time on the digital clock.

5. twenty-eight minutes after four
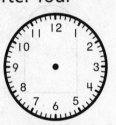

6. six forty-five

7. quarter to seven

Write the time as minutes *after* an hour and minutes *before* an hour.

8.
_____

_____

9.
_____

_____

10.
_____

_____

Remembering

Solve.

1. A theater has 8 rows of 9 seats. All the seats but 3 are full. How many people are in the audience? _____

2. Gil's scrapbook had 12 pages, each with 4 hockey cards in it. He gave 6 hockey cards to his brother. How many cards did Gil have left? _____

3. Odessa made 10 model cars with 4 wheels each. She had 8 wheels left over. How many wheels did she start with? _____

Draw all the possible lines of symmetry on each figure.

4.

5.
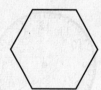

6.

Which two figures in each row are congruent?

7. Figures _____ and _____ are congruent.

  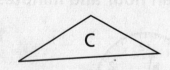 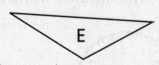

8. Figures _____ and _____ are congruent.

 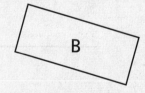 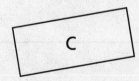

Homework

Complete.

1. What is the tenth month of the year? _____

2. What is the third month of the year? _____

3. What is the month 6 months before September? _____

4. What is the month 2 months after April? _____

5. What is the date 5 days after February 12? _____

6. What is the date 1 week before June 18? _____

7. What is the date 3 weeks after October 4? _____

8. July 2 to July 27 is _____ days.

9. November 21 to November 24 is _____ days.

10. Complete the table.

Start Time	Elapsed Time	End Time
2:00 P.M.		10:00 P.M.
2:27 A.M.		4:45 A.M.
3:30 A.M.	1 hour and 22 minutes	
2:10 P.M.	3 hours and 16 minutes	
	2 hours and ten minutes	11:00 A.M.
	4 hours and 39 minutes	7:53 P.M.

11. In July, Mark calculated that it would take him 6 months to save enough money to buy a skateboard. With his birthday money, he was able to buy the skateboard 1 month early. In what month did he buy the skateboard?

_____

Name _____ **Date** _____

Remembering

Write the unknown number.

1. $\boxed{} \times 8 = 24$

2. $28 \div 4 = \boxed{}$

3. $6 \times \boxed{} = 42$

4. $5 \times 7 = \boxed{}$

5. $\frac{40}{8} = \boxed{}$

6. $\boxed{} * 8 = 16$

7. $36 / 6 = \boxed{}$

8. $9 \bullet \boxed{} = 72$

9. $49 / 7 = \boxed{}$

Solve.

10. Clarence had 27 fish in one tank. He had twice as many fish in a second tank. He moved 12 fish from the second tank to the first one. How many fish are in the second tank? _____

11. Talia is saving for a ski trip. She saved $24 in January. In February, she saved twice as much. Her parents gave her another $30. How much money did she have altogether? _____

Find the area and perimeter of each figure.

12.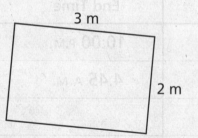

3 m

2 m

Perimeter = _____
Area = _____

13.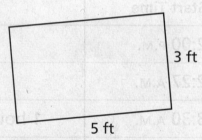

3 ft

5 ft

Perimeter = _____
Area = _____

14.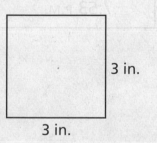

3 in.

3 in.

Perimeter = _____
Area = _____

15.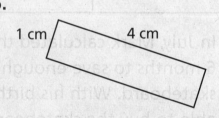

1 cm   4 cm

Perimeter = _____
Area = _____

Elapsed Time

Name _____ **Date** _____

Homework

These clocks show the movement of the minute hand.

Tell how many minutes have passed and how many degrees the minute hand has rotated.

1.   2.   3.    4.

minutes: _____   minutes: _____   minutes: _____   minutes: _____

degrees: _____   degrees: _____   degrees: _____   degrees: _____

The minute hand rotates 6 degrees(°) in one minute.

Complete.

5. From 3:33 to 3:42, _____ minutes pass.
   The minute hand rotates _____ degrees.

6. From 12:03 to 12:15, _____ minutes pass.
   The minute hand rotates _____ degrees.

7. From 1:57 to 2:08, _____ minutes pass.
   The minute hand rotates _____ degrees.

Solve.

8. A clock starts at 5:05. What time is it after the minute hand rotates 12°?

   _____

9. A clock starts at 12:59. What time is it after the minute hand rotates 24°?

   _____

10. A clock starts at 8:44. What time is it after the minute hand rotates 48°?

   _____

11. A clock starts at 1:00. What time is it after the minute hand rotates 36°?

   _____

Name _____ **Date** _____

Remembering

Find the missing number.

1. $7 \times 4 =$ ☐   **2.** $49 \div 7 =$ ☐   **3.** ☐ $* 6 = 54$

4. $24 / 6 =$ ☐   **5.** $9 \bullet$ ☐ $= 27$ **6.** $49 / 7 =$ ☐

7. ☐ $\times 5 = 45$ **8.** ☐ $/ 4 = 8$ **9.** $5 \times$ ☐ $= 40$

Complete the Missing Number Puzzle.

10.

×	5	4	
	30		54
9		36	
	35		

11.

×		8	
6			42
8			56
	21	56	

Write two letter names for each figure.

12.

_____

13.

_____

14.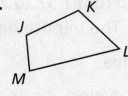

Draw each figure if possible.

15. A rectangle that is not a square.

16. A parallelogram that is not a rectangle.

17. A quadrilateral that is not a parallelogram.

18. A rhombus that is not a parallelogram.

Clock Angles

Sol~~ve each~~ **problem.**   *Show your work.*

1. One fourth of the fish in a tank are goldfish. There are 20 fish in the tank. How many are goldfish?

_____

2. One ninth of Ramon's books are mysteries. Ramon has 81 books. How many are mysteries?

_____

3. Dana has 48 socks. One eighth of Dana's socks are green. How many socks are green?

_____

Use mental math to find the answer.

4. $\frac{1}{3} \times 6 =$ _____   5. $\frac{1}{2} \times 14 =$ _____   6. $\frac{1}{6}$ of $24 =$ _____

7. $\frac{1}{4} \times 16 =$ _____   8. $\frac{1}{5} \times 30 =$ _____   9. $\frac{1}{7}$ of $49 =$ _____

Write each equation in two other ways.

10. $\frac{1}{8}$ of $24 = 3$ 11. $\frac{1}{5} \times 35 = 7$ 12. $15 \div 3 = 5$

_____   _____   _____

_____   _____   _____

Name _____ **Date** _____

Remembering

Multiply or divide.

1. $7 \times 3 =$ _____

2. $9 \times 9 =$ _____

3. $35 \div 7 =$ _____

4. $9 \times 3 =$ _____

5. $28 \div 4 =$ _____

6. $56 \div 8 =$ _____

7. $6 \times 7 =$ _____

8. $24 \div 8 =$ _____

9. $49 \div 7 =$ _____

10. $6 \times 6 =$ _____

11. $30 \div 5 =$ _____

12. $8 \times 8 =$ _____

Tell whether each pair of lines is parallel, perpendicular, or neither.

13.

14.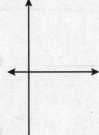

15.

16.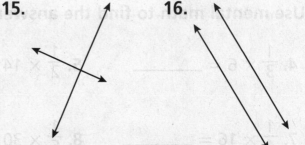

_____

_____

_____

17.

18.

19.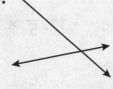

20.

_____

_____

_____

_____

Unit Fractions of Sets and Numbers

Homework

Name _____ **Date** _____

Use the bar graph at the right to fill in the blanks.

Number of Blocks Walked to School

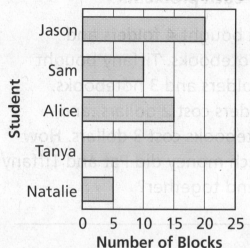

1. Sam walks _____ as many blocks as Natalie walks. Natalie walks _____ as many blocks as Sam walks.

2. Alice walks _____ as many blocks as Natalie walks. Natalie walks _____ as many blocks as Alice walks.

3. Sam walks _____ as many blocks as Jason walks. Jason walks _____ as many blocks as Sam walks.

4. Natalie walks _____ as many blocks as Tanya walks. Tanya walks _____ as many blocks as Natalie walks.

5. Jason walks _____ as many blocks as Natalie walks. Natalie walks _____ as many blocks as Jason walks.

Solve each problem.

6. Wanda picked 27 apples at the Sunshine Farm. Her little brother Roy picked $\frac{1}{3}$ as many apples. How many apples did Roy pick?

_____

7. Frankie has 7 baseball cards. Rika has 4 times as many baseball cards. How many baseball cards does Rika have?

_____

Name _____ **Date** _____

Remembering

Solve each problem.

1. Pat bought 4 folders and 3 notebooks. Tiffany bought 2 folders and 3 notebooks. Folders cost 2 dollars, and notebooks cost 3 dollars. How much money did Pat and Tiffany spend together?

_____

2. There are 3 pencils in an art box. There are 2 times as many markers as pencils. There are 3 times as many crayons as markers. How many pencils, markers, and crayons are in the box?

_____

3. Marge bought 3 books of stamps. There were 9 stamps in each book. Then her mom gave her 46 stamps, and her dad gave her 12 stamps. She used 5 stamps to mail letters. How many stamps does Margaret have left?

_____

4. Ilia walked 4 miles on Monday. He walked 3 times as far on Tuesday. On Tuesday, Anna walked half as far as Ilia walked on Tuesday. How far did Anna walk on Tuesday?

_____

Draw hands on the analog clock. Write the time on the digital clock.

5. half-past 12

6. eight-twenty

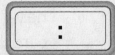

7. six-fifty

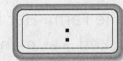

Compare with Fractions

Homework

Use the bar graph at the right to fill in the blanks.

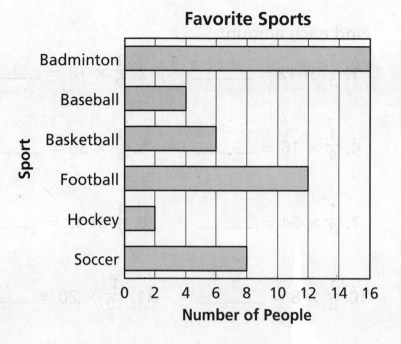

Favorite Sports

1. _____ as many people like hockey as like soccer. _____ as many people like soccer as like hockey.

2. _____ as many people like soccer as like badminton.

_____ as many people like badminton as like soccer.

3. _____ times as many people like football as like basketball. _____ as many people like basketball as like football.

4. _____ as many people like hockey as like football.

_____ as many people like football as like hockey.

5. _____ as many people like badminton as like hockey.

_____ as many people like hockey as like badminton.

Solve each problem.

6. There are 6 frogs in Swan Pond. There are 8 times as many frogs in Turtle Pond. How many frogs are in Turtle Pond?

_____

7. Last night Nigel counted 56 shooting stars. Tonight he counted $\frac{1}{7}$ as many. How many shooting stars did Nigel count tonight?

_____

Practice Fractional Comparisons **265**

Remembering

Find each amount.

1. $\frac{1}{3}$ of 12 = _____

2. $\frac{1}{6} \times 18$ = _____

3. $\frac{1}{7}$ of 35 = _____

4. $\frac{1}{4} \times 16$ = _____

5. $\frac{1}{6} \times 36$ = _____

6. $\frac{1}{9}$ of 81 = _____

7. $\frac{1}{8} \times 64$ = _____

8. $\frac{1}{7}$ of 42 = _____

9. $\frac{1}{5}$ of 25 = _____

10. $\frac{1}{8} \times 8$ = _____

11. $\frac{1}{10} \times 20$ = _____

12. $\frac{1}{4}$ of 4 = _____

lve each problem. If there is not enough
rmation to solve the problem, tell what else
would need to know.

Show your work.

13. e third graders went by bus to the science m seum. There were 27 students on one bus an 33 students on another bus. How many thir graders in all went to the science museum?

_____

14. Pietro has 8 stamps from Canada and some stamps from the United States. He has 72 stamps in all. How many stamps from the United States does Pietro have?

_____

15. Tracy has a lemonade stand. Today she sold $\frac{1}{9}$ as many cups of lemonade as she sold yesterday. How many cups of lemonade did Tracy sell today?

_____

Practice Fractional Comparisons

Name _____ **Date** _____

1. Danielle's parents bought some fruit for a family picnic. By the end of the picnic, $\frac{2}{6}$ of each type of fruit was eaten, and $\frac{4}{6}$ of each type was left. Complete the table to show how many of each type of fruit were eaten and how many were left.

Fruit Bought for the Picnic

	$\frac{2}{6}$ eaten	$\frac{4}{6}$ left
36 apples		
30 oranges		
48 peaches		
54 bananas		

Solve each problem.

2. Jorge has 72 books. Three eighths of his books are science fiction. How many of Jorge's books are science fiction?

_____

3. The Green Team scored 63 points at the spelling bee. Ranjit scored $\frac{2}{7}$ of the team's points. How many points did Ranjit score?

_____

Find each amount.

4. $\frac{2}{3}$ of 21 = _____

5. $\frac{5}{8} \times 16 =$ _____

6. $\frac{4}{9}$ of 27 = _____

7. $\frac{3}{7} \times 42 =$ _____

8. $\frac{4}{4} \times 20 =$ _____

9. $\frac{5}{6}$ of 36 = _____

Find a Fraction of a Set or a Number **267**

Name _____ **Date** _____

Remembering

Shade the figure to show the given fraction.
Then answer the question.

1. $\frac{4}{6}$

What part of the
rectangle is not
shaded?

_____

2. $\frac{3}{5}$

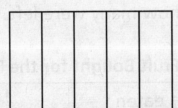

What part of the
rectangle is not
shaded?

_____

3. $\frac{1}{3}$

What part of the
rectangle is not
shaded?

_____

Answer each question.

4. What is the sixth month of the year?

_____

5. What is the month two months after July?

_____

6. What is the eleventh month?

_____

7. What is the month four months before
December?

_____

Find a Fraction of a Set or a Number

Homework

Complete.

1. Abbot and Maria baked 24 loaves of bread. Use the circle graph to complete the table.

Loaves of Bread Baked

$\frac{2}{6}$ white

$\frac{3}{8}$ wheat

$\frac{1}{6}$ banana

$\frac{1}{8}$ rye

	Fraction of Whole	Number of Loaves
White		
Rye		
Wheat		
Banana		

2. Did Abbot and Maria bake more banana or rye bread? How can you tell by looking at the graph?

_____

_____

_____

3. Aaron and his classmates have a total of 48 pets. Aaron made a circle graph to show the kinds of pets his classmates have. Write a fraction in the circle graph for each kind of pet.

4. How many more dogs are there than cats?

_____

Students' Pets

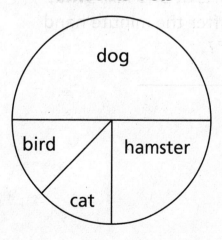

dog

bird

hamster

cat

Remembering

Find the area of each figure below.

1.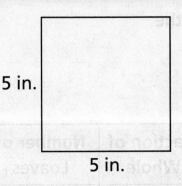

5 in.

5 in.

2.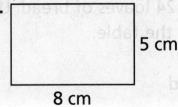

8 cm

5 cm

3.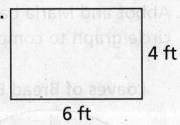

6 ft

4 ft

_____   _____   _____

4. Hal started his homework when he got home from school and worked until 4:45 P.M. He did homework for an hour and a half. What time did he start doing homework?

_____

5. Juanita practiced her flute from 3:30 to 4:00 P.M. each day Monday through Friday. How much time did she spend practicing her flute altogether on those days?

_____

6. A clock starts at 5:15 A.M. What time is it after the minute hand rotates 90°?

_____

7. It is 1:25 P.M. What time will it be when the minute hand rotates 180°?

_____

Homework

Look at the bag of marbles and use the words *impossible, certain, equally likely, likely,* or *unlikely* to describe the event of picking a marble out of the bag.

1. Pick a black marble _____

2. Pick a white marble _____

3. Pick a striped marble _____

4. Pick a marble _____

Use the bag of marbles above to complete. Write the probability in two ways.

5. What is the probability of picking a black marble? _____
   _____

6. What is the probability of picking a white marble? _____
   _____

7. What is the probability of picking a marble with dots? _____
   _____

8. What is the probability of picking a marble with stripes? _____
   _____

Look at the spinner, list the outcomes, and predict what you are more likely to spin.

9. _____   10. _____

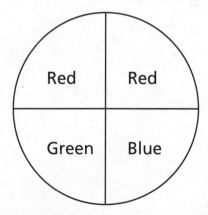

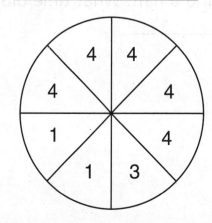

Remembering

Shade the figure to show the given fraction.

1. $\frac{2}{3}$

2. $\frac{3}{6}$

3. $\frac{1}{5}$

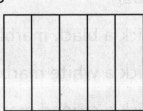

Find the area of each figure below.

4.
```
        3 in.
┌──────────────┐
│              │
│ 2 in.        │
│              │
└──────────────┘
```

5.
```
              7 ft
┌────────────────────────┐
│                        │
│ 4 ft                   │
│                        │
└────────────────────────┘
```

6.
```
      3 cm
┌──────────────┐
│              │
│              │
│ 5 cm         │
│              │
│              │
└──────────────┘
```

_____   _____   _____

Solve.

7. Harlem practiced soccer from 3:30 to 5:00 each day from Monday through Wednesday. How much time did he spend practicing soccer altogether on those days? _____

8. Ji finished watching the movie at 12:45 P.M. The movie lasted for an hour and a half. What time did Ji start watching the movie?

_____

Discover Probability

Homework

Use your fraction strips for exercises 1–6. Fill in the blanks.

1. How many twelfths are in one fourth? _____

   Complete these equations:

   _____ twelfths = 1 fourth $\dfrac{\square}{12} = \dfrac{1}{4}$

2. How many sixteenths are in one fourth? _____

   Complete these equations:

   _____ sixteenths = 1 fourth $\dfrac{\square}{16} = \dfrac{1}{4}$

3. How many eighths are in three fourths? _____

   Complete these equations:

   _____ eighths = 3 fourths $\dfrac{\square}{8} = \dfrac{3}{4}$

4. How many twelfths are in three fourths? _____

   Complete these equations:

   _____ twelfths = 3 fourths $\dfrac{\square}{12} = \dfrac{3}{4}$

5. How many sixteenths are in three fourths? _____

   Complete these equations:

   _____ sixteenths = 3 fourths $\dfrac{\square}{16} = \dfrac{3}{4}$

6. Find three other pairs of equivalent fractions.

_____   _____   _____

Name _____ **Date** _____

Remembering

Complete each Missing Number puzzle.

1.

×		7	6
5	40		
6			
		63	

2.

×	9	6	
7			
4			32
	27		

Flowers at the Flower Shop

3.

	$\frac{1}{5}$ white	$\frac{4}{5}$ not white
30 roses		
35 tulips		
45 carnations		
40 daisies		
20 lilies		

Items at the Clothing Store

4.

	$\frac{1}{8}$ blue	$\frac{7}{8}$ not blue
72 shirts		
24 jackets		
64 pairs of pants		
48 skirts		
56 caps		

Introduce Equivalence

Play *Spinning a Whole* with a friend or with a member of your family. Use the game boards and spinners that your teacher gave you. Here are the rules.

Rules for *Spinning a Whole*

Number of Players: 2 or 3

Materials: a game board and matching pair of spinners for each player, paper clips, ruler

1. On each turn, a player chooses and spins one of the two spinners.

2. Using the labeled fraction bars as a guide, the player marks and shades a section of the whole to represent the fraction the spinner landed on.

   - On a player's first turn, the player starts at the left end of the whole.
   - On other turns, the player starts at the right end of the last section shaded.

3. If a player spins a fraction greater than the unshaded portion of the whole, the player does not shade anything on his or her turn.

4. The first player to fill his or her whole bar completely and exactly wins.

Use the fraction bars on the *Spinning a Whole* game boards to fill in the blanks.

1. $\dfrac{1}{4} = \dfrac{\boxed{}}{16}$

2. $\dfrac{1}{2} = \dfrac{\boxed{}}{8}$

3. $\dfrac{5}{8} = \dfrac{\boxed{}}{16}$

4. $\dfrac{1}{3} = \dfrac{\boxed{}}{6}$

5. $\dfrac{5}{6} = \dfrac{\boxed{}}{12}$

6. $\dfrac{2}{3} = \dfrac{\boxed{}}{12}$

Name _____ **Date** _____

Remembering

Add or subtract.

1. $2.77
    + 4.25

2. 348
    + 867

3. 340
    − 209

4. $8.36
    + 9.41

5. $3.60
    − 2.17

6. 739
    + 279

7. 724
    − 687

8. $7.38
    − 4.45

Solve each problem.

Show your work.

> Chip earned $17 washing cars. His brother Dirk earned $32 raking leaves.

9. How much more money must Chip earn to have as much as Dirk?

_____

10. Dirk spent $\frac{1}{2}$ of his money on some new CDs. How much money does Dirk have now?

_____

> There are 3 black horses on the big merry-go-round, and 7 times as many white horses. There are 6 black horses on the small merry-go-round, and 4 times as many white horses.

11. Which merry-go-round has more white horses?

_____

12. How many more white horses does it have?

_____

Explore Equivalence

Use the fraction strips to show how each pair is equivalent.

1. $\frac{1}{3}$ and $\frac{2}{6}$

$$\frac{1}{3} = \frac{1 \times \boxed{}}{3 \times \boxed{}} = \frac{2}{6}$$

2. $\frac{3}{4}$ and $\frac{9}{12}$

$$\frac{3}{4} = \frac{3 \times \boxed{}}{4 \times \boxed{}} = \frac{9}{12}$$

3. $\frac{2}{5}$ and $\frac{4}{10}$

$$\frac{2}{5} = \frac{2 \times \boxed{}}{5 \times \boxed{}} = \frac{4}{10}$$

4. $\frac{2}{4}$ and $\frac{6}{12}$

$$\frac{2}{4} = \frac{2 \times \boxed{}}{4 \times \boxed{}} = \frac{6}{12}$$

Complete to show how the fractions are equivalent.

5. $\frac{5}{6}$ and $\frac{35}{42}$

$$\frac{5}{6} = \frac{5 \times \boxed{}}{6 \times \boxed{}} = \frac{35}{42}$$

6. $\frac{4}{7}$ and $\frac{36}{63}$

$$\frac{4}{7} = \frac{4 \times \boxed{}}{7 \times \boxed{}} = \frac{36}{63}$$

Complete.

7. $\frac{4}{9} = \frac{4 \times \boxed{}}{9 \times \boxed{}} = \frac{\boxed{}}{45}$

8. $\frac{2}{5} = \frac{2 \times \boxed{}}{5 \times \boxed{}} = \frac{\boxed{}}{40}$

9. $\frac{3}{8} = \frac{3 \times \boxed{}}{8 \times \boxed{}} = \frac{18}{\boxed{}}$

Name _____ **Date** _____

Remembering

Draw the next figure in the pattern.

1.

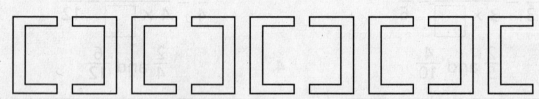

2.

3.

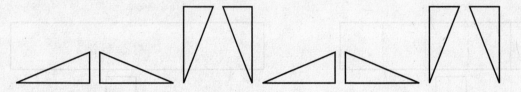

4.

Complete each Missing Number puzzle.

5.

×	6		7
9		72	
	24		28
	18	24	21

6.

×	8		
7		28	63
5	40		45
	24	12	

Find Equivalent Fractions by Multiplying

Homework

Use grouping to show that the fractions are equivalent.

1. $\dfrac{6}{9}$ and $\dfrac{2}{3}$

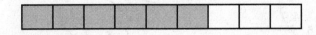

$$\dfrac{6}{9} = \dfrac{6 \div \square}{9 \div \square} = \dfrac{2}{3}$$

2. $\dfrac{9}{12}$ and $\dfrac{3}{4}$

$$\dfrac{9}{12} = \dfrac{9 \div \square}{12 \div \square} = \dfrac{3}{4}$$

3. $\dfrac{12}{20}$ and $\dfrac{3}{5}$

$$\dfrac{12}{20} = \dfrac{12 \div \square}{20 \div \square} = \dfrac{3}{5}$$

4. $\dfrac{16}{24}$ and $\dfrac{2}{3}$

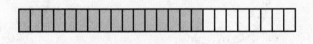

$$\dfrac{16}{24} = \dfrac{16 \div \square}{24 \div \square} = \dfrac{2}{3}$$

Simplify.

5. $\dfrac{10}{60} = \dfrac{10 \div \square}{60 \div \square} = \dfrac{\square}{6}$

6. $\dfrac{9}{45} = \dfrac{9 \div \square}{45 \div \square} = \dfrac{1}{\square}$

7. $\dfrac{27}{36} = \dfrac{27 \div \square}{36 \div \square} = \dfrac{\square}{4}$

8. $\dfrac{20}{24} = \dfrac{20 \div \square}{24 \div \square} = \dfrac{\square}{6}$

9. $\dfrac{14}{21} = \dfrac{14 \div \square}{21 \div \square} = \dfrac{2}{\square}$

10. $\dfrac{16}{40} = \dfrac{16 \div \square}{40 \div \square} = \dfrac{2}{\square}$

11. $\dfrac{24}{64} = \dfrac{24 \div \square}{64 \div \square} = \dfrac{\square}{8}$

12. $\dfrac{16}{72} = \dfrac{16 \div \square}{72 \div \square} = \dfrac{2}{\square}$

13. $\dfrac{24}{42} = \dfrac{24 \div \square}{42 \div \square} = \dfrac{\square}{7}$

Name _____ **Date** _____

Remembering

Write each time in numbers. Then write each time in words.

1.

_____

_____

2.

_____

_____

3.

_____

_____

4.

_____

_____

5.

_____

_____

6.

_____

_____

Complete the table.

7.

Start Time	Elapsed Time	End Time
9:05 A.M.		9:55 A.M.
10:30 A.M.	2 hours, 30 minutes	
	4 hours, 30 minutes	3:25 P.M.
7:05 P.M.	5 hours, 15 minutes	
4:25 P.M.		8:30 P.M.
7:10 A.M.	3 hours, 45 minutes	

Find Equivalent Fractions by Dividing

Homework

Add. Use fraction strips to help if you need to.

1. $\frac{2}{8} + \frac{3}{8} =$ _____

2. $\frac{5}{16} + \frac{3}{16} =$ _____

3. $\frac{3}{7} + \frac{4}{7} =$ _____

4. $\frac{2}{3} + \frac{2}{12} =$ _____

| $\frac{2}{3}$ | $\frac{2}{12}$ |

$\frac{\square}{12} + \frac{2}{12} = \frac{\square}{12}$

Add twelfths.

5. $\frac{2}{4} + \frac{3}{12} =$ _____

| $\frac{2}{4}$ | $\frac{3}{12}$ |

$\frac{\square}{12} + \frac{3}{12} = \frac{\square}{12}$

Add twelfths.

6. $\frac{3}{10} + \frac{2}{5} =$ _____

| $\frac{3}{10}$ | $\frac{2}{5}$ |

$\frac{3}{10} + \frac{\square}{10} = \frac{\square}{10}$

Add tenths.

7. $\frac{1}{3} + \frac{2}{5} =$ _____

| $\frac{1}{3}$ | $\frac{2}{5}$ |

$\frac{\square}{15} + \frac{\square}{15} = \frac{\square}{15}$

Add fifteenths.

8. $\frac{2}{4} + \frac{3}{8} =$ _____

| $\frac{2}{4}$ | $\frac{3}{8}$ |

Add _____.

9. $\frac{2}{3} + \frac{1}{4} =$ _____

| $\frac{2}{3}$ | $\frac{1}{4}$ |

Add _____.

10. $\frac{2}{6} + \frac{2}{4} =$ _____

| $\frac{2}{6}$ | $\frac{2}{4}$ |

Add _____.

11. $\frac{3}{9} + \frac{1}{6} =$ _____

| $\frac{3}{9}$ | $\frac{1}{6}$ |

Add _____.

12. $\frac{1}{6} + \frac{2}{4} =$ _____

| $\frac{1}{6}$ | $\frac{2}{4}$ |

Add _____.

Remembering

Write the equivalent fractions shown in the drawing.

1.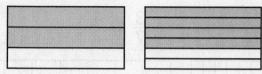

2.

_____ = _____   _____ = _____

3.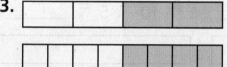

4.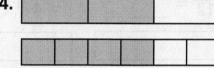

_____ = _____   _____ = _____

5.

6.

_____ = _____   _____ = _____

7.

8.

_____ = _____   _____ = _____

Solve.

9. Jane's mother baked 25 cookies. Jane ate $\frac{2}{5}$ of them. How many did she eat?

_____

10. Ali has 28 math problems. He has finished $\frac{5}{7}$ of them. How many problems has Ali finished?

_____

Add Any Fractions

Name _____ **Date** _____

Homework

Compare. Write >, <, or = in the ◯. Use fraction strips if you need to.

1. $\frac{1}{2}$ ◯ $\frac{1}{3}$ 2. $\frac{1}{4}$ ◯ $\frac{1}{5}$ 3. $\frac{2}{5}$ ◯ $\frac{4}{5}$

4. $\frac{5}{5}$ ◯ $\frac{4}{6}$ 5. $\frac{3}{8}$ ◯ $\frac{2}{4}$ 6. $\frac{2}{6}$ ◯ $\frac{1}{3}$

Write the fractions in order from greatest to least.

7. $\frac{1}{3}, \frac{1}{6}, \frac{1}{5}$ 8. $\frac{2}{6}, \frac{1}{6}, \frac{5}{6}$ 9. $\frac{2}{3}, \frac{2}{4}, \frac{2}{5}$

_____   _____   _____

Add, compare, and subtract each pair of fractions.

	Add	Compare	Subtract
10.	$\frac{1}{6} + \frac{1}{3} =$ _____	$\frac{1}{6}$ ◯ $\frac{1}{3}$	
11.	$\frac{2}{5} + \frac{1}{2} =$ _____	$\frac{2}{5}$ ◯ $\frac{1}{2}$	
12.	$\frac{3}{8} + \frac{1}{8} =$ _____	$\frac{3}{8}$ ◯ $\frac{1}{8}$	

Solve.

13. In Kayla's marble collection, $\frac{1}{4}$ of the marbles are blue and $\frac{3}{8}$ are red. Are there more blue marbles or red marbles? Explain.

_____

Name _____ **Date** _____

Remembering

Multiply or divide.

1. $49 \div 7 = \boxed{}$

2. $42 / 6 = \boxed{}$

3. $8\overline{)56}$ $\boxed{}$

4. $8 \times 7 = \boxed{}$

5. $6 \times 6 = \boxed{}$

6. $48 \div 8 = \boxed{}$

7. $7\overline{)42}$ $\boxed{}$

8. $72 \div 8 = \boxed{}$

9. $6 * 8 = \boxed{}$

10. $7 \cdot 6 = \boxed{}$

11. $8\overline{)72}$ $\boxed{}$

12. $36 / 6 = \boxed{}$

Mark all the words that describe each triangle.

13.

☐ equilateral
☐ isosceles
☐ scalene
☐ right
☐ acute
☐ obtuse

14.

☐ equilateral
☐ isosceles
☐ scalene
☐ right
☐ acute
☐ obtuse

15.

☐ equilateral
☐ isosceles
☐ scalene
☐ right
☐ acute
☐ obtuse

16.

☐ equilateral
☐ isosceles
☐ scalene
☐ right
☐ acute
☐ obtuse

Compare and Subtract Fractions

Homework

Write each fraction as a decimal

1. $\frac{2}{10}$ = _____   **2.** $\frac{8}{100}$ = _____   **3.** $\frac{75}{100}$ = _____

Write each decimal as a fraction

4. 0.9 = _____   **5.** 0.3 = _____   **6.** 0.35 = _____

Write an equivalent decimal.

7. 0.1 = _____   **8.** 0.40 = _____   **9.** 0.30 = _____   **10.** 0.9 = _____

Write >, < or = in the ◯ **.**

11. $0.45 ◯ $0.60   **12.** 0.6 ◯ 0.25   **13.** $0.75 ◯ $0.55

Write these amounts in order from least to greatest.

14. $\frac{1}{2}$ dollar, $0.55, $0.25   **15.** $\frac{1}{4}$ of a dollar, $0.10, $0.45   **16.** 0.85, 0.82, 0.8

_____   _____   _____

17. Kali has 10 ballons. 3 are red. Write a decimal
that represents the number of red balloons as
a part of all the balloons. _____

Name _____   **Date** _____

Remembering

Complete.

1. $\dfrac{3}{4} = \dfrac{3 \times \square}{4 \times \square} = \dfrac{\square}{12}$

2. $\dfrac{2}{3} = \dfrac{2 \times \square}{3 \times \square} = \dfrac{6}{\square}$

3. $\dfrac{7}{8} = \dfrac{7 \times \square}{8 \times \square} = \dfrac{\square}{\square}$

4. $\dfrac{2}{5} = \dfrac{2 \times \square}{5 \times \square} = \dfrac{\square}{10}$

5. $\dfrac{1}{6} = \dfrac{1 \times \square}{6 \times \square} = \dfrac{2}{\square}$

6. $\dfrac{3}{5} = \dfrac{3 \times \square}{5 \times \square} = \dfrac{\square}{\square}$

Find the perimeter of each figure below.

7.
3 in.

2 in.

_____

8.
7 ft

4 ft

_____

9.
3 cm

5 cm

_____

Multiply or divide to find the unknown number.

10. $8 \times \square = 64$

11. $35 \div 7 = \square$

12. $\square \bullet 7 = 42$

13. $\square / 6 = 8$

14. $9\overline{)\square}^{\,8}$

15. $9 \times \square = 81$

Fractions and Decimals

Name _____ **Date** _____

Write the mixed number and improper fraction that each drawing shows.

1.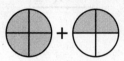

$$1 \quad + \quad \underline{\quad} \quad = \quad \underline{\quad}$$

$$\frac{4}{4} \quad + \quad \underline{\quad} \quad = \quad \underline{\quad}$$

2.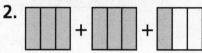

$$1 \quad + \quad \underline{\quad} \quad + \quad \underline{\quad} \quad = \quad \underline{\quad}$$

$$\frac{3}{3} \quad + \quad \underline{\quad} \quad + \quad \underline{\quad} \quad = \quad \underline{\quad}$$

3.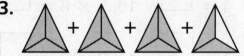

$$1 \quad + \quad \underline{\quad} \quad + \quad \underline{\quad} \quad + \quad \underline{\quad} \quad = \quad \underline{\quad}$$

$$\frac{3}{3} \quad + \quad \underline{\quad} \quad + \quad \underline{\quad} \quad + \quad \underline{\quad} \quad = \quad \underline{\quad}$$

4.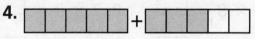

$$1 \quad + \quad \underline{\quad} \quad = \quad \underline{\quad}$$

$$\underline{\quad} \quad + \quad \underline{\quad} \quad = \quad \underline{\quad}$$

Write the improper fraction or mixed number.

5. $\frac{13}{7} = $ _____

6. $1\frac{2}{5} = $ _____

7. $\frac{8}{3} = $ _____

8. $2\frac{3}{7} = $ _____

9. $\frac{13}{5} = $ _____

10. $3\frac{5}{9} = $ _____

11. $\frac{19}{4} = $ _____

12. $2\frac{1}{6} = $ _____

Name   **Date**

Remembering

Add or subtract.

1. $\$1.14$
    $+ \ 3.67$

2. 192
    $+ 479$

3. 518
    $- 371$

4. $\$5.52$
    $+ \ 4.48$

5. $\$4.44 - \$1.81 =$ _____

6. $724 - 68 =$ _____

Multiply or divide.

7. $9 \times 8 = \boxed{}$

8. $7 \times 3 = \boxed{}$

9. $4 \times 4 = \boxed{}$

10. $5 \times 8 = \boxed{}$

11. $6 \times 3 = \boxed{}$

12. $4 \times 7 = \boxed{}$

13. $9 \times 2 = \boxed{}$

14. $8 \times 7 = \boxed{}$

Solve.

15. Elijah had $20. He spent $\frac{1}{2}$ of the money on paint and $\frac{1}{4}$ of it on art paper. How much money does he have left

_____

16. James ate $\frac{3}{8}$ of a pizza. Joyce ate $\frac{1}{4}$ of the pizza. What fraction of the pizza did they eat together?

_____

17. Chaka drank $\frac{3}{4}$ of a glass of lemonade. Shana drank $\frac{7}{8}$ of a glass of lemonade. Who drank more lemonade? How much more?

_____

18. There was a party in Mr. Spector's class. Jonelle brought $\frac{1}{2}$ of the cookies and Raya brought $\frac{1}{3}$ of the cookies. Who brought more cookies?

_____

     Explore Improper Fractions and Mixed Numbers

Name _____ **Date** _____

Homework

Write the answer.

1. $6\overline{)44}$ **2.** $4\overline{)29}$ **3.** $5\overline{)42}$ **4.** $9\overline{)47}$

5. $7\overline{)59}$ **6.** $4\overline{)34}$ **7.** $7\overline{)63}$ **8.** $9\overline{)57}$

9. $8\overline{)70}$ **10.** $4\overline{)28}$ **11.** $7\overline{)67}$ **12.** $6\overline{)40}$

Solve.

13. Gus is making valentines. He needs 6 paper hearts for each one. He has 55 hearts. How many valentines can he make? How many paper hearts will be left over?

_____

14. Felipe is gathering the soccer balls after the team's practice. There are 32 balls. Each sack holds 7 balls. How many sacks does Felipe need to gather all the balls?

_____

15. Ashley is putting ice cubes into glasses before dinner. There are 46 ice cubes. Each glass holds 6 ice cubes. How many glasses can she fill completely? How many ice cubes will be left over?

_____

16. The Outdoor Club is planning a canoe trip. There are 31 people in the club. Each canoe can hold 4 people. How many canoes does the club need to rent for the trip?

_____

Remembering

Add, compare, and subtract each pair of fractions.

	Add	Compare	Subtract
1.	$\frac{1}{6} + \frac{3}{4} =$ _____	$\frac{1}{6} \bigcirc \frac{3}{4}$	
2.	$\frac{2}{8} + \frac{1}{4} =$ _____	$\frac{2}{8} \bigcirc \frac{1}{4}$	
3.	$\frac{3}{7} + \frac{1}{2} =$ _____	$\frac{3}{7} \bigcirc \frac{1}{2}$	
4.	$\frac{4}{5} + \frac{1}{10} =$ _____	$\frac{4}{5} \bigcirc \frac{1}{10}$	
5.	$\frac{1}{3} + \frac{3}{8} =$ _____	$\frac{1}{3} \bigcirc \frac{3}{8}$	

Find the area of each figure.

6.

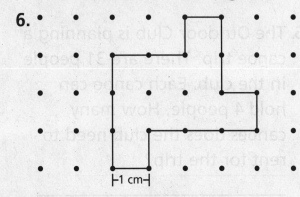

7.

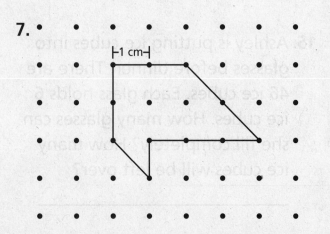

Homework

Write the quotient with a remainder or as a mixed number.

1. $7\overline{)37}$ 2. $8\overline{)78}$ 3. $6\overline{)49}$ 4. $3\overline{)19}$

5. $7\overline{)52}$ 6. $6\overline{)54}$ 7. $7\overline{)67}$ 8. $8\overline{)70}$

9. $6\overline{)40}$ 10. $9\overline{)38}$ 11. $8\overline{)64}$ 12. $7\overline{)25}$

Solve.

13. The third-graders at Coburn School won a recycling contest. The 4 third-grade classes get to share 38 pizzas equally. How much pizza does each class get?

_____

14. David has 70 cans of paint to pack into crates. Each crate holds 8 cans of paint. How many crates will David need to pack all the paint?

_____

15. Mabel has 45 stickers. She can fit 10 stickers on each page. How many pages will she fill completely? How many stickers will be left?

_____

16. The 8 soccer players of the Middle School soccer team will share 20 bottles of water equally. How much water will each player get?

_____

Remembering

Find the missing number.

1. $56 \div 7 = \boxed{}$

2. $7 * \boxed{} = 63$

3. $3\overline{)36}$

4. $81 \div \boxed{} = 9$

5. $\boxed{}\overline{)48}$ $\overset{6}{}$

6. $4 \cdot 7 = \boxed{}$

7. $\overset{\boxed{}}{4\overline{)32}}$

8. $72 \div \boxed{} = 9$

9. $\boxed{} \times 4 = 12$

10. $\boxed{} \div 6 = 4$

11. $6 \times \boxed{} = 12$

12. $56 / \boxed{} = 8$

Find the measure of the unknown angle.

13.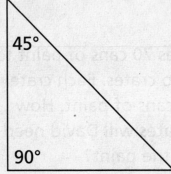

14.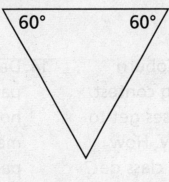

15.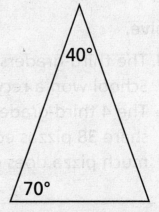

_____

_____

16. Jonathan has $\frac{1}{5}$ as many markers as Sheila. Sheila has 25 markers. How many markers does Jonathan have?

_____

17. The Tigers won 20 baseball games this season. The Hawks won $\frac{3}{4}$ as many games. How many games did the Hawks win?

_____

   Understand Remainders

Write the answer with a remainder and as a mixed number.

1. $68 \div 8$ _____

2. $41 \div 7$ _____

3. $82 \div 9$ _____

4. $38 \div 4$ _____

5. $57 \div 7$ _____

6. $78 \div 8$ _____

7. $49 \div 8$ _____

8. $40 \div 6$ _____

Solve.

9. Emma's father is building her a dollhouse. Each room can hold 6 dolls. If Emma has 38 dolls, how many rooms does her father need to build in the doll house?

_____

10. Mamie is baking cupcakes for her 7 cousins. She wants to divide the cupcakes equally among her cousins. If Mamie bakes 45 cupcakes, how many whole cupcakes will each cousin get? What part of a cupcake will each cousin get?

_____

11. Monica has 39 pieces of tape. She needs 4 pieces to hang 1 poster. How many posters can she hang? How many pieces of tape will she have left over?

_____

12. Mr. Chavez made 19 pies for his 4 neighbors. If the neighbors share the pies equally, how much pie will each neighbor get?

_____

Remembering

Solve.

1. Betty and Jake hit baseballs at the batting cage. Betty's first hit flew 81 feet. Jake's ball went $\frac{1}{9}$ as far. How many feet did Jake's ball travel?

_____

2. Roberto and Jayla weighed some candy. Roberto had 6 pounds, and Jayla had $\frac{2}{3}$ as much. How many pounds of candy did Jayla have?

_____

3. Tyrone bought a sweater that cost $26.99. Then he bought a coat that cost twice as much. How much did he spend in all?

_____

4. A carpenter has two screws. One is $\frac{1}{2}$ inch long and the other is $\frac{7}{8}$ inch long. How much longer is one screw than the other?

_____

Which two figures in each row are congruent?

5.

6.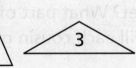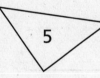

_____

7.

_____

Connections

Write a word problem that has fractions in it. Give the answer to the problem.

_____

_____

_____

_____

_____

_____

Reasoning and Proof

Chen has 14 pens. Dave says he has exactly $\frac{1}{3}$ the number of pens that Dave has. Is that possible? Explain.

_____

_____

_____

_____

_____

Communication

Are $\frac{2}{3}$ and $\frac{4}{6}$ equivalent fractions? Explain.

_____

_____

_____

_____

_____

Representation

What is the difference between *4 times as many as 8* and $\frac{1}{4}$ *as many as 8*? Draw a picture to show the difference.

_____

_____

Remembering

Solve.

1. Pedro has a board that is 42 inches long. Otis has a board that is $\frac{1}{6}$ of that length. How long is Otis's board? _____

2. Kaya has blue ribbon and red ribbon. The blue ribbon is $\frac{3}{4}$ inches wide and the red ribbon is $\frac{1}{2}$ inch wide. How much wider is one ribbon than the other?

   _____

3. Jennifer spent $50.50 for a pair of shoes. Then she bought a skirt that cost half as much? How much did she spend in all? _____

4. Shing has green apples and red apples. The red apples weigh 8 pounds. The green apples weigh $\frac{3}{4}$ as much. How much do the green apples weigh? _____

Find the measure of the unknown angle.

5.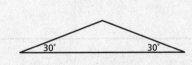

_____

6.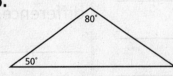

_____

7.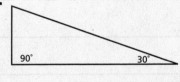

_____

Find the missing number.

8. $36 \div \boxed{} = 9$ **9.** $8 \times 8 = \boxed{}$ **10.** $45 \div 9 = \boxed{}$

Use Mathematical Processes

Name _____ **Date** _____

Homework

Circle the nets you predict will form a cube. Use extra paper to draw and test one of your predictions.

1.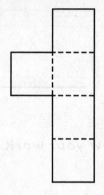

2.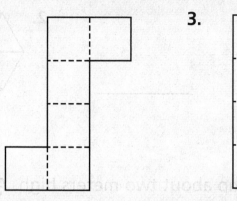

3.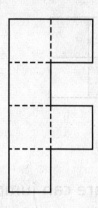

4.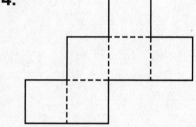

5.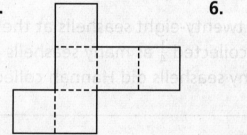

6.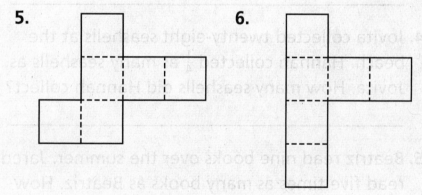

7. On grid paper, draw a different net that will form a cube when it is cut out and folded.

Explore Cubes **301**

Name _____ **Date** _____

Remembering

Write a fraction to represent the shaded portion of the figure.

1. _____

2. _____

Solve.

Show your work.

3. A hare can jump about two meters high. A tiger can jump twice as high. How many meters high can a tiger jump?

_____

4. Jovita collected twenty-eight seashells at the beach. Hannah collected $\frac{1}{4}$ as many seashells as Jovita. How many seashells did Hannah collect?

_____

5. Beatriz read nine books over the summer. Jared read five times as many books as Beatriz. How many books did Jared read?

_____

Write the time in numbers and write two ways to say the time.

6.

7.

8.

_____   _____   _____

_____   _____   _____

Explore Cubes

Name   **Date**

Homework

Use the model for exercises 1–2.

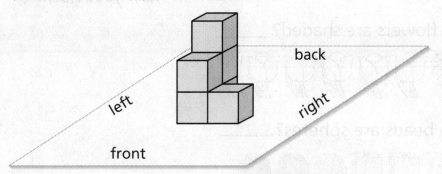

1. Draw the top view of the model.

2. Label each view of the model as *front, back, right,* or *left.*

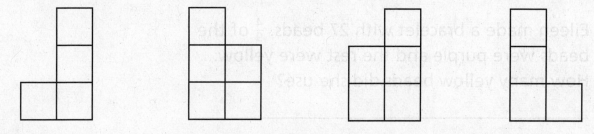

_____   _____   _____   _____

Use the model below for exercise 3.

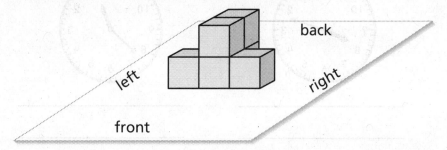

3. Draw the *front, back, right,* and *left* views of the model.

     front   **back**   **left**   **right**

Remembering

Solve. *Show your work.*

1. What fraction of the flowers are shaded? _____

2. What fraction of the beads are spheres? _____

3. Mitchell built 15 cars from blocks. He put wheels on $\frac{2}{5}$ of them. On how many cars did he put wheels?

_____

4. Eileen made a bracelet with 27 beads. $\frac{4}{9}$ of the beads were purple and the rest were yellow. How many yellow beads did she use?

_____

Write the time in numbers. Then write two ways to say the time.

5.

6.

7.

_____   _____   _____

_____   _____   _____

_____   _____   _____

Write the time in numbers.

8. twelve past six

9. seven twenty-four

_____   _____

Two-Dimensional Pictures of Three-Dimensional Buildings

Homework

Name the solid figure. List some real-world items that have the same shape.

1.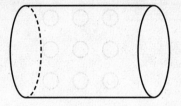

_____

_____

_____

2.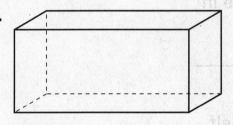

_____

_____

_____

3.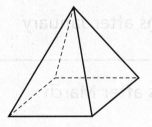

_____

_____

Name _____ **Date** _____

Remembering

Shade the given fraction.

1. $\frac{3}{4}$

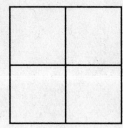

2. $\frac{5}{7}$

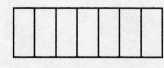

3. $\frac{5}{9}$

Solve.

4. There are 56 horses on a farm. One eighth of them are in the barn. How many horses are in the barn?

_____

5. One sixth of the books on Alan's shelf are about Egypt. There are 24 books on the shelf. How many books on the shelf are about Egypt?

_____

Find the month.

6. Three months after April

_____

7. Three months after January

_____

8. Seven months after May

_____

9. Nine months after March

_____

10. Two months after December

_____

11. Four months before August

_____

Explore Prisms, Cylinders, and Pyramids

Homework

Name each solid figure. Write other things that are this shape.

1.

_____

_____

2.

_____

_____

3.

_____

_____

Draw the shape of a package you could use to ship a telescope.

4.

Name _____ **Date** _____

Remembering

Use mental math.

1. $\frac{1}{4} \times 4 =$ _____

2. $\frac{1}{2} \times 8 =$ _____

3. $\frac{1}{3} \times 12 =$ _____

Write each equation two other ways.

4. $\frac{1}{4}$ of $12 = 3$

5. $16 \div 4 = 4$

6. $\frac{3}{7} \times 21 = 9$

_____

_____

_____

_____

_____

_____

Solve.

Show your work.

7. Vanya organized 27 photos into an album. Four photos fit on each page. How many pages did she use? How many photos were on the page that was not full?

_____

8. Michel had 38 marbles. He gave 9 marbles to each player. How many players were there? How many marbles were left over?

_____

Write the time as minutes after an hour and minutes before an hour.

9.

10.

11.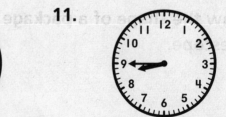

_____

_____

_____

_____

_____

_____

Explore Cones

Homework

1. Place a pencil inside one end of a large paper clip. Hold the pencil point in place on this sheet of paper. Place another pencil inside the other end of the paper clip. Ask your Homework Helper to hold your paper still while you draw a circle by moving the second pencil. Label one radius, one diameter, and the circumference.

2. Name three spheres that you might see every day.

   _____

3. Give one example of how a sphere is similar to a circle.

   _____

4. Give one example of how a sphere is different from a circle.

   _____

Remembering

Solve.

1. How many fourths are in one half? _____

2. _____ fourths = 1 half

3. $\dfrac{\boxed{}}{4} = \dfrac{1}{2}$

4. How many twelfths are in one third? _____

5. _____ twelfths = 1 third

6. $\dfrac{\boxed{}}{12} = \dfrac{1}{3}$

Solve.   *Show your work.*

7. A chef is preparing meals for 8 dinner guests. She has cooked 32 small potatoes. Each plate will have an equal number of potatoes. How many potatoes will she put on each plate?

   _____

8. A pastry chef is making blackberry pies and a blackberry crumble. He has nineteen cups of blackberries. Each pie uses three cups of blackberries. If he makes five pies, how many cups of blackberries will he have for the crumble?

   _____

Fill in the blanks.

9. From 6:36 to 6:51, _____ minutes pass, and the

   minute hand rotates _____ degrees.

10. From 6:15 to 6:45, _____ minutes pass, and the

    minute hand rotates _____ degrees.

Explore Circles and Spheres

Name _____ **Date** _____

Homework

> **1 foot (ft) = 12 inches (in.)**
> **1 yard (yd) = 3 ft or 36 in.**
> **1 mile (mi) = 5,280 ft or 1,760 yd**

Complete.

1. 1 foot 5 inches = _____ inches

2. 1 yard 8 inches = _____ inches

3. 2 feet 1 inch = _____ inches

4. 1 yard 2 feet = _____ inches

5. 2 yards 2 inches = _____ inches

6. 3 feet 5 inches = _____ inches

7. 9 feet = _____ yards

8. 15 feet = _____ yards

9. 19 feet = _____ yards _____ foot or _____ yards

10. 22 feet = _____ yards _____ foot or _____ yards

11. 14 feet = _____ yards _____ feet or _____ yards

12. Write the name of an object that is about 3 yards long.

_____

13. Write the name of an object that is about 2 inches long.

_____

14. Write the name of an object that is about 2 feet long.

_____

Choose the unit you would use to measure each.
Write _inch_, _foot_, _yard_, or _mile_.

15. the length of a lizard

_____

16. the distance to from your house to the library

_____

17. the height of the ceiling

_____

Remembering

Write the equivalent fractions.

1.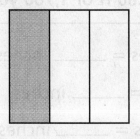

_____ = _____

2.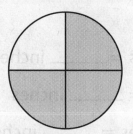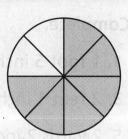

_____ = _____

3.

_____ = _____

Solve.

4. Tomás picked 28 pumpkins from his pumpkin patch. He shared them with his 3 sisters. Each of the 4 children got the same number of pumpkins. How many pumpkins did each child get?

_____

5. On the first day of the fair, 781 people rode the Screamer roller coaster. 432 more people rode the Screamer on the last day of the fair than on the first day. How many people rode the Screamer on the last day?

_____

6. At a yard sale, books are 50¢ each. Jess wants to buy as many as possible with a $10 bill. How many books can he buy?

_____

7. Josephine swam two miles every day for two weeks at the health club. How many miles did she swim in all?

_____

Inches, Feet and Yards

Homework

Estimate the length of each line segment. Then measure it to the nearest centimeter.

1. ————————————

   Estimate: _____ Actual: _____

|⊢—⊣|
1 cm

2. ——————

   Estimate: _____ Actual: _____

3. ——————————

   Estimate: _____ Actual: _____

Complete the tables.

4.

m	cm
1	
2	
	500
8	
10	

5.

m	dm
1	
	50
	60
8	
9	

6.

dm	m
10	
20	
40	
	8
	10

7. Describe a distance that is about 3 meters long.

   _____

Choose the unit you would use to measure each. Write *centimeter*, *decimeter*, *meter*, or *kilometer*.

8. the height of a chair _____

9. the distance you can throw a ball _____

10. the distance you could walk in half an hour _____

Name _____   **Date** _____

Remembering

Use the graph to answer the questions below.

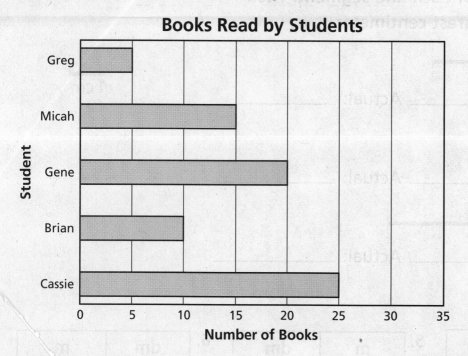

Books Read by Students

1. Micah read _____ as many books as Greg.

   Greg read _____ as many books as Micah.

2. Cassie read _____ as many books as Greg.

   Greg read _____ as many books as Cassie.

3. Gene read _____ as many books as Brian.

   Brian read _____ as many books as Gene.

Solve.

4. Julia wants to give some books to 6 of her friends. She has 38 books to give away. How many books will each friend receive? How many books will be left over?

   _____

5. A grocer is packing oranges into boxes of 10. If he has 98 oranges, how many boxes will he need to pack all the oranges? _____

Centimeters, Decimeters, and Meters

Homework

> 1 cup (c) = 8 fluid ounces (fl oz)
> 2 cups (c) = 1 pint (pt)
> 4 cups (c) = 1 quart (qt)
> 16 cups (c) = 1 gallon (gal)

Solve.

1. A recipe calls for 4 pints of milk. How many times must a 1-cup measuring cup be filled to equal 4 pints?

   _____

2. Leroy has 2 containers. The blue container holds 12 cups. The red container holds 5 pints. Which container holds more? How much more?

   _____

Complete.

3. 12 cups = _____ pints

4. _____ cups = 5 pints

5. 16 cups = _____ quarts

6. 32 fluid ounces = _____ gallon

7. _____ pints = 12 quarts

8. _____ quarts = 5 gallons

9. 12 quarts = _____ gallons

10. 13 pints = _____ quarts

11. _____ fluid ounces = $\frac{1}{4}$ quart

12. _____ quarts = 6 gallons

13. 16 pints = _____ gallons

14. 7 pints = _____ quarts

Choose the best unit to measure how much each item can hold. Write *cup, pint, quart,* or *gallon.*

15. a bathtub _____

16. a container of orange juice _____

17. a juice box _____

18. a small milk carton _____

Remembering

Divide.

1. 6)$\overline{30}$

2. 28 / 7 _____

3. 86 ÷ 9 _____

4. 4)$\overline{23}$

5. 38 / 4 _____

6. 12 ÷ 2 _____

7. 73 / 8 _____

8. 17 ÷ 3 _____

9. 26 ÷ 4 _____

10. 6)$\overline{56}$

11. 46 ÷ 8 _____

12. 52 / 5 _____

Solve.

13. At a Superbowl party, there was a 26 foot submarine sandwich for 8 people to eat. How many feet of the submarine sandwich did each person eat if all the people ate an equal amount of the sandwich?

_____

14. Cheryl and Ami want to buy a present for their teacher that costs $53.80. Since they don't have enough money, they ask some friends to join them. What is the fewest number of friends they need to ask so each pays less than $7.00?

_____

Write the name of the 3-D figure.

15.

_____

16.

_____

17.

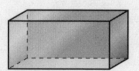

_____

18.

_____

Customary Units of Capacity

Homework

> **1 liter (L) = 1,000 milliliters (mL)**

Complete.

1. 4,000 mL = _____ L   **2.** $3\frac{1}{2}$ L = _____ mL   **3.** 750 mL = _____ L

4. _____ L = 6,500 mL   **5.** _____ mL = $2\frac{1}{4}$ L   **6.** 6,000 mL = _____ L

Complete.

7.

L	mL
2	
3	
$4\frac{1}{2}$	
$5\frac{1}{4}$	
$6\frac{3}{4}$	

8.

mL	L
250	
1,750	
2,500	
7,000	
8,500	

Circle the better estimate.

9. a container of milk   2 L   20 mL   **10.** a horse   6 kg   600 kg

11. an eyedropper   1 L or 1 mL   **12.** a banana 6 lb   6 oz

Choose the unit you would use to measure the capacity of each. Write *mL* or *L*.

13. a container of glue _____   **14.** an aquarium _____

Solve.

15. Diana had a 1-liter container of water. She drank half of the water in the container. How many milliliters of water does she have left?

_____

16. A scientist has 150 milliliters of a liquid. How many 10-milliliter test tubes does she need to hold all the liquid?

_____

Name _____ **Date** _____

Remembering

Solve.

1. An art teacher has 20 pounds of clay for a group of 9 students. How much clay will each student receive?

_____

2. Allen has 64 cans of soup to pack into crates. Each crate holds 7 cans of soup. How many crates will Allen need to pack all the soup?

_____

3. Teresa has 39 stamps. She wants to give an equal amount of stamps to each of 6 friends. How many stamps can she give each friend? How many stamps will be left over?

_____

_____

4. There are 34 yards of fabric on a roll. If 6 yards are needed to make a dress, how many dresses can be made with the fabric?

_____

What solid figure does the net make?

5.

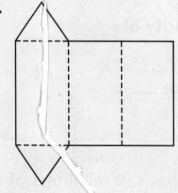

6.

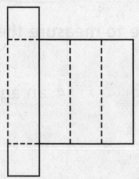

7.

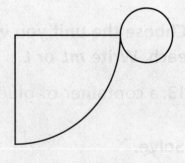

_____

_____

_____

Metric Units of Capacity

Name _____ **Date** _____

Homework

Write the improper fraction or mixed number.

1. $\frac{6}{4}$ c = _____ c

2. $\frac{8}{6}$ ft = _____ ft

3. $\frac{12}{7}$ qt = ____ qt

4. $1\frac{5}{6}$ ft = ____ ft

5. $1\frac{1}{3}$ c = ____ c

6. $2\frac{1}{5}$ gal = ____ gal

7. $\frac{10}{3}$ gal = ____ gal

8. $\frac{12}{5}$ yd = ____ yd

9. $1\frac{5}{6}$ ft = ____ ft

10. $\frac{8}{5}$ mi = ____ mi

11. $\frac{5}{3}$ c = ____ c

12. $2\frac{4}{7}$ mi = ____ mi

13. $\frac{15}{12}$ ft = _____ ft

14. $7\frac{2}{3}$ yd = ____ yd

15. $4\frac{3}{4}$ ft = ____ ft

Write the length of each line segment using an improper fraction and a mixed number.

16. _____

17. _____

18. _____

Name _____ **Date** _____

Remembering

Divide. If there is a remainder, give the answer as a mixed number.

1. 54 / 2 _____   **2.** 82 ÷ 4 _____   **3.** 30 ÷ 6 _____

4. 24 ÷ 12 _____   **5.** 58 ÷ 3 _____   **6.** 45 / 7 _____

7. 73 ÷ 8 _____   **8.** 36 / 3 _____   **9.** 43 / 9 _____

10. 19 ÷ 2 _____   **11.** 37 ÷ 5 _____   **12.** 48 / 2 _____

Solve.

13. At the right is a diagram of George's rock garden. He wants to put a fence around it. How much fencing does he need? The fencing costs $10 per foot. Use mental math to find the total cost.

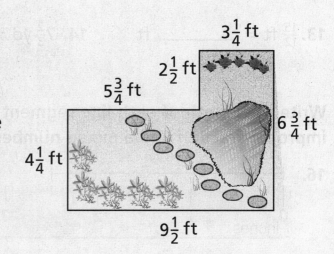

$3\frac{1}{4}$ ft

$2\frac{1}{2}$ ft

$5\frac{3}{4}$ ft

$6\frac{3}{4}$ ft

$4\frac{1}{4}$ ft

$9\frac{1}{2}$ ft

_____

14. Mrs. Lee wants to put tile on the floor of her kitchen. Each tile covers 1 square foot. How many tiles does she need to cover the floor? Each tile costs $3. Use mental math to find the total cost.

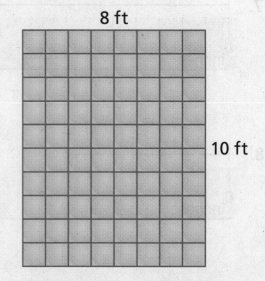

8 ft

10 ft

_____

Improper Fractions and Mixed Numbers in Measurements

Homework

inches (in.)	centimeter (cm)
feet (ft)	decimeter (dm)
yard (yd)	cup (c)
quart (qt)	gallon (gal)

Complete.

1.

in.	yd
36	1
1	$\frac{1}{36}$
6	
9	

2.

dm	m
10	1
1	
2	
5	

3.

cm	dm
10	1
1	
6	
11	

4.

c	qt
4	1
1	
	2
12	

5.

pt	gal
8	1
1	
4	
	$1\frac{1}{8}$

6.

qt	gal
4	1
3	
1	
	$1\frac{3}{4}$

7. 36 in. = _____ ft = _____ yd

8. 12 in. = _____ ft = _____ yd

9. 6 in. = _____ ft = _____ yd

10. 18 in. = _____ ft = _____ yd

11. Teresa drank 2 quarts of water on her hiking trip. Josh drank $\frac{1}{4}$ gallon of water. What fraction of a gallon did they drink in all? Show your work.

_____

Measurement Equivalencies and Fractions **325**

Name _____ **Date** _____

Remembering

Estimate the length of each line segment in inches.
Then measure it to the nearest $\frac{1}{2}$ inch.

1. _____

   Estimate: _____ Actual: _____

2. _____

   Estimate: _____ Actual: _____

3. _____

   Estimate: _____ Actual: _____

Estimate the length of each line segment in inches. Then
measure it to the nearest $\frac{1}{4}$ inch.

4. _____

   Estimate: _____ Actual: _____

5. _____

   Estimate: _____ Actual: _____

6. _____

   Estimate: _____ Actual: _____

7. _____

   Estimate: _____ Actual: _____

Solve.

8. Nicholas is on the track team.
   He ran $\frac{3}{4}$ of a mile on Monday.
   He ran $\frac{7}{12}$ of a mile on Tuesday.
   On which day did he run
   farther?

   _____

9. Each week, Joy spends $\frac{3}{8}$ of her
   allowance on baseball cards
   and $\frac{1}{4}$ of her allowance on
   snacks. Does Joy spend more
   for baseball cards or snacks?

   _____

Measurement Equivalencies and Fractions

Name _____ **Date** _____

Homework

Choose the unit you would use to measure the weight of each object. Write *ounce* or *pound*.

1.

_____

2.

_____

3.

_____

Choose the unit you would use to measure the mass of each object. Write *gram* or *kilogram*.

4.

_____

5.

_____

6.

_____

Circle the better estimate.

7. a pillow   8 oz   8 lb   8. a stapler   250 g   250 kg

9. a car   1,000 g   1,000 kg   10. a large book   3 lb   30 lb

Complete.

11.

Ounces	16	2				12
Pounds	1		$\frac{4}{16}$ or $\frac{1}{4}$	2	$\frac{1}{2}$	

12.

Grams	1,000		3,000			5
Kilograms	1	$\frac{3}{1,000}$		5	$\frac{1}{2}$	

Solve.

13. Michael has 1 pound of ground turkey to make 4 turkey burgers of the same weight. How many ounces should he put in each turkey burger?

_____

Name _____ **Date** _____

Remembering

Complete.

1. $1\frac{1}{2}$ in. $+ 3\frac{6}{8}$ in.

_____

2. $7\frac{3}{4}$ in. $+ \frac{3}{8}$ in.

_____

3. $3\frac{1}{4}$ in. $+ 7\frac{3}{8}$ in.

_____

4. $4\frac{3}{4}$ in. $+ 7\frac{1}{2}$ in.

_____

Complete.

5. 13 ft = _____ yd

6. 13 ft = _____ in.

7. 8 yd = _____ ft

8. 20 cm = _____ dm

9. 20 dm = _____ m

10. 4 m = _____ cm

11. 11 pt = _____ qt

12. 7 qt = _____ gal

13. 4 c = _____ fl oz

14. 8 L = _____ mL

15. 750 mL = _____ L

16. 5,500 mL = _____ L

Complete the table.

17.

Start Time	Elapsed Time	End Time
10:05 A.M.		10:55 P.M.
11:30 A.M.	2 hours, 30 minutes	
	4 hours, 30 minutes	2:15 P.M.
8:25 P.M.	5 hours, 15 minutes	

Customary Units of Weight and Metric Units of Mass

Homework

Name

Date

HOT
100°C
water
boils

C   F
100   220
            210
90   200
            190
80   180
            170
70   160
            150
HOT   140
40°C   13
a very   12
hot day   11
           HOT
40   104°F
           a very
WARM   hot day
20°C   100
room   90
temp.   80
30   70
           WARM
20   70°F
           room
COOL   temp.
10°C   60
a day   COOL
when you   50°F
need a   50 a day
jacket   40 when you
           30 need a
10   20 jacket
0   10
COOL   0
0°C   COLD
water   32°F
freezes   water
-10   -10 freezes
-20   -20
-30

Circle the better estimate for the temperature.

1.

10°F   75°F

2.

25°F   55°F

3.

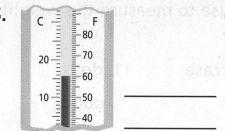

32°C   100°C

4.

2°C   20°C

Write the temperature using °F. Then write hot, warm, cool, or cold to describe the temperature.

5.

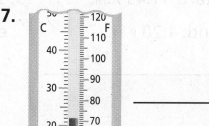

C   F
           80
20   70
           60
10   50
           40

_____

_____

6.

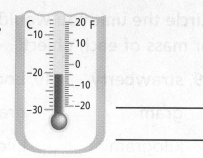

C   -10   20 F
            10
     -20   0
            -10
     -30   -20

_____

_____

Write the temperature using °C. Then write hot, warm, cool, or cold to describe the temperature.

7.

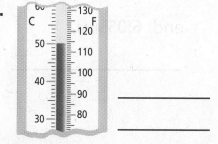

50   120
C   110
40 F
           100
30   90
           80
20   70

_____

_____

8.

60   130
C   120
50 F   110
           100
40   90
30   80

_____

_____

Remembering

Circle the unit you would use to measure the length of each object.

1. table	2. pencil	3. eraser	4. doorway
inch	inch	centimeter	centimeter
foot	foot	meter	meter
mile	yard	kilometer	kilometer

Circle the unit you would use to measure the capacity of each object.

5. baby bottle	6. spoon	7. milk carton	8. bathtub
cup	milliliter	milliliter	cup
quart	liter	liter	quart
gallon			gallon

Circle the unit you would use to measure the weight or mass of each object.

9. strawberry	10. bookcase	11. dog	12. quarter
gram	gram	ounce	ounce
kilogram	kilogram	pound	pound

Find the elapsed time.

13. start: 5:20 A.M.

    end: 6:05 A.M.

14. start: 11:45 A.M.

    end: 1:20 P.M.

15. start: 7:25 P.M.

    end: 9:15 P.M.

_____   _____   _____

Connections

Write a word problem that involves measurement. Give the answer to the problem.

_____

_____

_____

_____

_____

Reasoning and Proof

Support or disprove the following statement. A net of a cube is always made up of 6 squares.

_____

_____

_____

_____

_____

Communication

How is a cone like a square pyramid? How is it different?

_____

_____

_____

_____

Representation

Show the fraction $\frac{3}{4}$ on a number line. Show the fraction $\frac{2}{3}$ on a number line. Use the number lines to explain which fraction is greater.

_____

_____

_____

_____

_____

_____

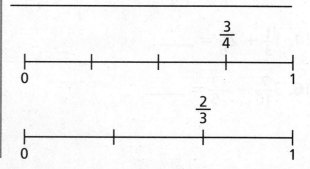

Remembering

Circle the unit you would use to measure the length of each object.

1. pen	2. window	3. shoe	4. car
inch	inch	centimeter	centimeter
foot	foot	meter	meter
yard	mile	kilometer	kilometer

Circle the unit you would use to measure the weight or mass of each object.

5. nickel	6. horse	7. desk	8. nail
gram	ounce	gram	ounce
kilogram	pound	kilogram	pound

Find the elapsed time.

9. start: 2:40 P.M.
end: 3:15 P.M.

_____

10. start: 11:15 A.M.
end: 12:40 P.M.

_____

11. start: 9:25 A.M.
end: 11:15 A.M.

_____

Complete.

12. $3\frac{1}{2} + 2\frac{5}{8} =$ _____

13. $2\frac{3}{4} + \frac{5}{8} =$ _____

14. $1\frac{1}{3} + 2\frac{5}{6} =$ _____

15. $2\frac{2}{5} + 3\frac{3}{5} =$ _____

16. $3\frac{7}{10} + 4\frac{3}{5} =$ _____

17. $2\frac{5}{6} + 5\frac{1}{2} =$ _____

Use Mathematical Processes

Name _____ **Date** _____

Homework

This is a map of the animals in a zoo.

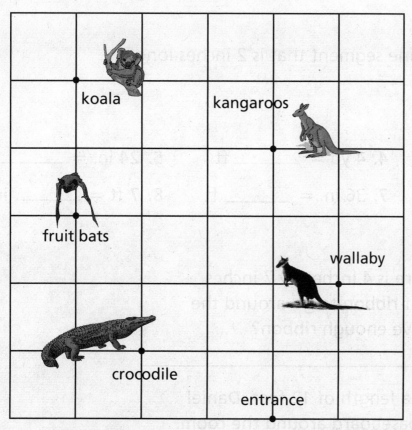

1. If you start at the entrance and walk 3 units up and
   3 units left, where will you be? _____

2. Which is closer to the koala, the kangaroo or the
   fruit bats? _____

3. Describe a route from the fruit bats to the wallaby.

   _____

4. Choose two places on the map. Describe two routes
   from one place to the other. Which route is longer?

   _____

   _____

   _____

Remembering

1. Draw a horizontal line segment that is 4 inches long.

2. Draw a horizontal line segment that is 2 inches long.

Complete.

3. 3 ft = _____ in.   **4.** 4 yd = _____ ft   **5.** 24 in. = _____ ft

6. 6 yd = _____ ft   **7.** 36 in. = _____ ft   **8.** 7 ft = _____ in.

Solve.

9. A rectangular picture is 4 inches by 7 inches. Elmore has 2 feet of ribbon to go around the picture. Does he have enough ribbon?

_____

10. A square room has a length of 12 feet. Daniel wants to put new baseboard around the room. How many yards of baseboard does he need?

_____

Circle the nets that you think will form a cube when folded. Copy the nets onto paper and cut them out. Fold them to test your predictions.

11.    **12.**    **13.**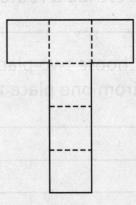

Use the coordinate grid below for exercises 1–10.

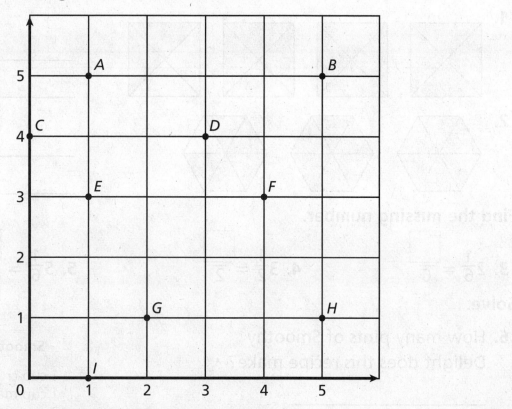

Write the ordered pair for each point.

1. *E* (_____, _____)

2. *H* (_____, _____)

3. *G* (_____, _____)

4. *B* (_____, _____)

Write the letter of the point for each ordered pair.

5. (1, 0) _____

6. (4, 3) _____

7. (3, 4) _____

8. (1, 5) _____

9. (0, 4) _____

10. (5, 1) _____

11. Mark the following ordered pairs on the grid.
(1, 1) (1, 4) (4, 1) (4, 4)

12. Draw a line segment to connect the points in order
that you marked for exercise 11. Name the figure.

_____

Remembering

Write an improper fraction and a mixed number for the shaded part.

1.

_____

_____

2.

_____

_____

Find the missing number.

3. $2\frac{1}{6} = \frac{\square}{6}$

4. $3\frac{1}{2} = \frac{\square}{2}$

5. $5\frac{1}{6} = \frac{\square}{\square}$

Solve.

6. How many pints of Smoothy Delight does this recipe make?

_____

7. Jill has a 12-cup punch bowl. How many quarts will it hold?

_____

Smoothy Delight
1 cup crushed ice
1 cup mashed banana
2 cups peach juice
1 cup rice milk

Complete.

8. Name the solid figure shown at the right.

_____

9. Sketch a net that will make this solid.

10. List three objects in the shape of this solid.

_____

Locate Points on a Coordinate Grid

Homework

1. Mark a point on this coordinate grid to form the third vertex of an acute triangle.

2. Write the ordered pair for each vertex.

   (_____, _____) (_____, _____) (_____, _____)

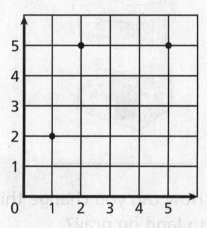

3. Mark a point on this coordinate grid to form the fourth vertex of a parallelogram. Join the four points to make a parallelogram.

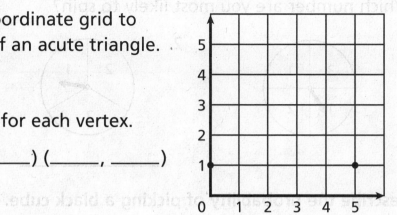

4. Write the ordered pair for each vertex.

   (_____, _____) (_____, _____)

   (_____, _____) (_____, _____)

5. Draw a rectangle on this coordinate grid with a width that is 2 units shorter than its length.

6. Write the ordered pair for each vertex.

   (_____, _____) (_____, _____)

   (_____, _____) (_____, _____)

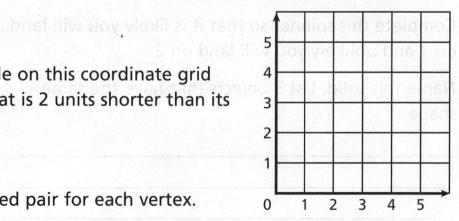

Name _____ **Date** _____

Remembering

Which number are you most likely to spin?

1.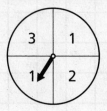

_____

2.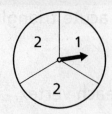

_____

3.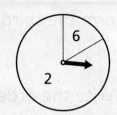

_____

Describe the probability of picking a black cube.
Use the words _certain_, _likely_, _unlikely_, or _impossible_.

4.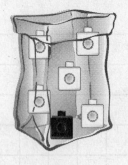

_____

5.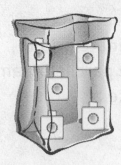

_____

6.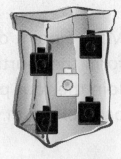

_____

7. How can you change this spinner to make it certain to land on gray?

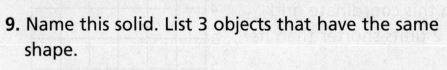

_____

_____

8. Complete this spinner so that it is likely you will land on 1 and unlikely you will land on 2.

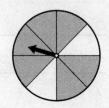

9. Name this solid. List 3 objects that have the same shape.

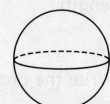

_____

_____

Explore Line Segments and Figures on a Coordinate Grid

Homework

Write the value of the underlined digit.

1. 98,<u>7</u>65 _____ **2.** 88,<u>2</u>65 _____ **3.** 9,50<u>6</u> _____ **4.** <u>6</u>7,894 _____

Write each number in standard form.

5. twenty five thousand, eight hundred thirty _____

6. ninety nine thousand, six hundred nine _____

Write each number in word form.

7. 8,013 _____

8. 13,456 _____

Write greater than (>), less than (<), or equal (=) to make each statement true.

9. 8,652 ◯ 8,562   **10.** 9,001 ◯ 9,011

Write each group of numbers in order from least to greatest.

11. 567 2,346 765   **11.** 8,065 8,056 8,650

_____   _____

Solve using any method.

13. In a recent election, 17,285 people voted in one city and 26,122 voted in another city. How many people voted in both cities?

_____

14. On Saturday, the baseball stadium had 36,004 fans at the game. On Sunday they had 28,990. How many more fans were at Saturday's game than at Sunday's game?

_____

Name   Date

**15. Write the number 183,421 in word form. Then
write the place value name of the digit 8.**

_____

_____

_____

_____

_____

_____

_____

_____

_____

_____

_____

_____

_____

_____

_____

_____

_____

_____

Homework

1. Label the length and width (in units) of each rectangle.

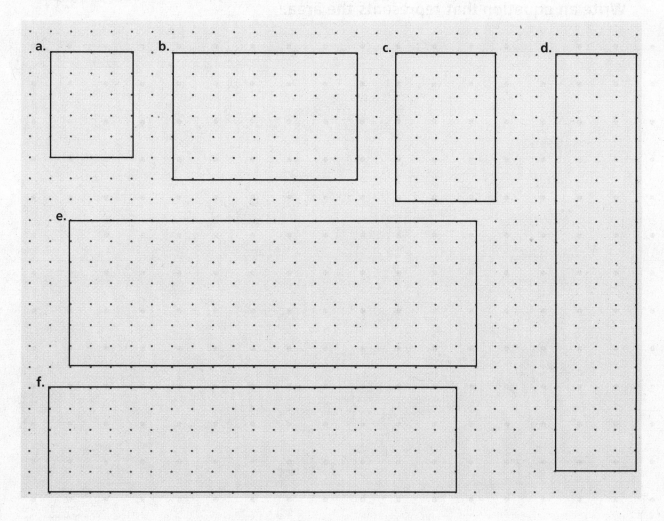

2. Write the equation representing the area (in square units) of each rectangle shown above.

a. _____   b. _____   c. _____

d. _____   e. _____   f. _____

Find the area (in square units) of a rectangle with the given dimensions.

3. $3 \times 4 =$ _____   **4.** $3 \times 40 =$ _____   **5.** $30 \times 40 =$ _____

Homework

6. Draw a rectangle with side lengths of 5 cm and 10 cm.
Write an equation that represents the area.

Homework

Find each product by factoring the tens. Draw rectangles if you need to.

1. 6×6, 6×60, and 60×60

_____

_____

2. 7×6, 70×6, and 70×60

_____

_____

3. 5×6, 5×60, and 50×60

_____

_____

4. 6×5, 60×5, and 60×50

_____

_____

5. 5×9, 50×9, and 50×90

_____

_____

6. 4×8, 4×80, and 40×80

_____

_____

On a sheet of grid paper, draw two different arrays of connected squares for each total. Label the sides and write the multiplication equation for each of your arrays.

7. 18 squares

_____

_____

8. 20 squares

_____

_____

9. 24 squares

_____

_____

Homework

10. Explain how you can multiply 4 × 100 using mental math.

_____

_____

_____

_____

_____

11. Explain how you can multiply 40 × 70 using mental math.

_____

_____

_____

_____

_____

Mental Math and Multiplication with Tens

Draw a rectangle. Find the tens product, the ones product, and the total product. The first one is done for you.

1. 5×29

$29 =$ 20 $+$ 9

5	$5 \times 20 = 100$	$5 \times 9 = 45$

$\begin{array}{r} 100 \\ + 45 \\ \hline 145 \end{array}$

2. 9×54

3. 7×32

4. 3×47

Solve each problem.

Show your work.

5. Adele's flower garden is 14 feet long and 3 feet wide. How many square feet is her garden?

_____

6. Adele planted 15 trays of flowers. Each tray had 7 flowers in it. How many flowers did she plant?

_____

7. Write and solve a multiplication word problem about your family.

_____

_____

_____

_____

Homework

8. Choose two factors that have a product of 104.
   Draw a quick picture to show that you are correct.
   You do not need to draw the area model actual
   size. Just make a sketch.

Model One-Digit by Two-Digit Multiplication

Use any method to solve. Sketch a rectangle model if you need to.

1. 8 × 54 _____

2. 5 × 76 _____

3. 6 × 82 _____

4. 57 × 7 _____

5. 6 × 63 _____

6. 36 × 9 _____

7. 5 × 93 _____

8. 4 × 65 _____

9. 27 × 8 _____

Solve each problem.

Show your work.

10. 74 people are sitting down to a fancy six-course meal. The first course is soup, which only needs a spoon. The rest of the courses each need fresh forks. How many forks will be used?

_____

11. Dawn is a traveling sign salesperson. She uses plastic letters to make the signs. A dress store chain asks Dawn to put signs in front of their 56 stores that say "SALE: HALF PRICE ON ALL DRESSES." How many plastic "S" letters will Dawn need?

_____

12. Find the product of 5 × 72.
Then explain which method you prefer to use.

_____

_____

_____

_____

_____

_____

_____

_____

_____

_____

_____

_____

_____

_____

_____

_____

_____

_____

Solve using any numeric method. Use rounding and estimating to see if your answer makes sense.

1. 82 × 6 _____

2. 7 × 43 _____

3. 9 × 38 _____

4. 2 × 94 _____

5. 4 × 68 _____

6. 81 × 6 _____

7. 35 × 9 _____

8. 5 × 79 _____

9. 2 × 74 _____

Solve each problem.

Show your work.

10. Describe how you solved one of the exercises above. Write at least two sentences.

_____

_____

_____

_____

_____

_____

11. Miranda wrote the full alphabet (26 letters) 6 times. How many letters did she write?

_____

12. Niko has 17 packs of bulletin-board cutouts. Each one contains 7 shapes. How many shapes does she have altogether?

_____

13. Explain how multiplication and addition are related.

_____

_____

_____

_____

_____

_____

_____

_____

_____

_____

_____

_____

_____

_____

_____

_____

_____

_____

_____

_____

Discuss Different Methods of Multiplication

Name _____ **Date** _____

Homework

Sketch rectangles and solve by any method that relates to your sketch.

1. 4 × 786 _____

2. 5 × 919 _____

3. 8 × 572 _____

4. 586 × 7 _____

5. Zack has 42 basketball cards in his collection. Morry has 7 times as many cards as Zack. How many basketball cards do Zack and Morry have together?

Show your work.

_____

6. Shari's grandmother lives about 800 miles away from her. Her mother's car can go about 350 miles on one tank of gasoline. How many times will Shari's mother have to fill the gas tank in order to drive to and from her grandmother's house?

_____

7. The soccer season lasts for 9 weeks. Lavonne's team practices 45 minutes on Saturdays. Jason's team practices 25 minutes on Mondays and on Thursdays. Which team practices more each week? How many more minutes do they practice during the season?

_____

8. Write and solve a multiplication word problem with a three-digit number.

_____

_____

_____

9. Explain how to multiply 4 × 382.

_____

_____

_____

_____

_____

_____

_____

_____

_____

_____

_____

_____

_____

_____

_____

_____

_____

_____

Homework

On a separate sheet of paper, sketch a rectangle for each problem and solve using any method. Round and estimate to check your answer.

1. 3 × 475 _____

2. 7 × 80 _____

3. 6 × 521 _____

4. 8 × 386 _____

5. Describe the steps you used for one of your solutions to exercises 1–4.

_____

_____

A third-grade class is counting the supplies in their art cupboard. Help them to finish their count.

Show your work.

6. They have 3 rolls of red craft paper. The paper on the rolls is 4 feet wide and 72 feet long. How many square feet of craft paper do they have altogether?

_____

7. They counted 88 boxes of colored pencils and 63 boxes of markers. If each box holds 8 pencils or markers, how many colored pencils and markers do they have altogether?

_____

8. They found 9 boxes of glass marbles. There are 376 marbles per box. How many glass marbles do they have in all?

_____

9. They found 3 full pads of sketching paper and another 64 loose sheets. If each full pad has 90 sheets of paper, how many sheets of sketching paper do they have in all?

_____

Homework

10. Write and solve a word problem using the factors 6 and 246.

_____

_____

_____

_____

_____

_____

_____

_____

_____

_____

_____

_____

_____

_____

_____

_____

_____

_____

Practice One-Digit by Three-Digit Multiplication

Homework

Solve using any method.

1. 5)440 _____

2. 5)270 _____

3. 6)330 _____

4. 5)220 _____

5. 5)310 _____

6. 4)260 _____

Solve.

Show your work.

7. A school ordered 300 balloons for math night.
The balloons were evenly packaged into
6 boxes. How many balloons were in each box?

_____

8. 125 prizes were ordered to give away at the fair. If
the souvenirs were evenly packaged in 5 bags,
how many souveniers came in each bag?

_____

9. Explain how to solve this problem.

How many six-packs of juice do you need to have
360 juice boxes?
Draw a picture if you need to.

_____

_____

_____

_____

_____

_____

_____

_____

_____

_____

_____

_____

_____

_____

_____

_____

Find the Unknown Factor

Name _____

Date _____

Estimate each product. Solve to check your estimate.

1. 2×92

_____

_____

2. 5×63

_____

_____

3. 6×93

_____

_____

4. 4×84

_____

_____

5. 4×26

_____

_____

6. 4×96

_____

_____

Use compatible numbers to estiimate each quotient.

7. $327 \div 4$

$\boxed{} \div \boxed{} = \boxed{}$

8. $625 \div 9$

$\boxed{} \div \boxed{} = \boxed{}$

9. $296 \div 6$

$\boxed{} \div \boxed{} = \boxed{}$

10. $727 \div 8$

$\boxed{} \div \boxed{} = \boxed{}$

Estimate and then solve each problem.

Show your work.

11. Tania's little sister read 65 pages for the Summer Reading Club. Tania read 8 times as many pages as her sister. How many pages did Tania read?

_____

12. The school library shows one book and one magazine each day in the display case. If the librarian has 27 books and 7 magazines to use for the display, how many days can a different pair be on display?

_____

13. Explain how to estimate the product for 3 × 129 using rounding.
Then explain how to estimate the product for 3 × 129 using compatible numbers.

_____

_____

_____

_____

_____

_____

_____

_____

_____

_____

_____

_____

_____

_____

_____

_____

_____

_____

_____

Name _____ **Date** _____

Solve using any method. _Show your work._

1. Jude had a package of 25 pencils. He bundled them in 5 groups with a rubber band. How many pencils were in each group? _____

2. Beverly had 6 vases of flowers. Each vase had 13 flowers in it. How many flowers did she have in all?

_____

3. Hector needs to count how many floor tiles there are in his bathroom. He counts 19 rows of tiles going across and 8 tiles going down one side. How many tiles does he have? _____

Show how to solve problems 1–3 in another way.

4.

5.

6.

7. Write and solve your own word problem.

_____

_____

_____

8. Show how to solve problem 7 in another way.

9. Explain how multiplication and division are related.

_____

_____

_____

_____

_____

_____

_____

_____

_____

_____

_____

_____

_____

_____

_____

_____

_____

_____

_____

Name _____ **Date** _____

Homework

Use the line graph below to answer the questions that follow.

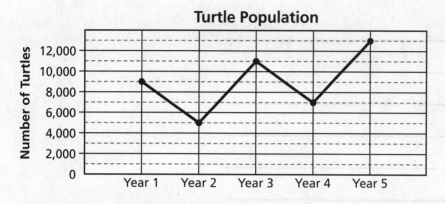

Turtle Population

1. The graph shows the turtle population at the end of each year during a 5-year period. What was the turtle population in Year 4?

   _____

2. How much greater was the population in Year 1 than in Year 2? _____

3. Which year represents the greatest turtle population? What was the population that year?

   _____

Make a line graph.

January	35°F
February	25°F
March	50°F
April	60°F

4. The cloud at the right shows average temperatures for 4 months. Make a line graph to show the data.

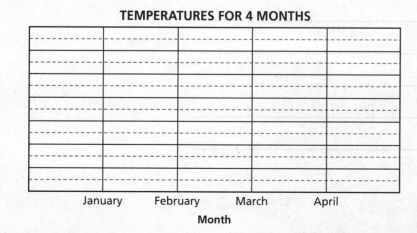

TEMPERATURES FOR 4 MONTHS

5. Write two questions and answers about your graph.

_____

_____

_____

_____

_____

_____

_____

_____

_____

_____

_____

_____

_____

_____

_____

_____

_____

_____

_____

_____